"Cecil Murphey has been the co of my books and is a tremendously powerful and persi once again, manifested in *The Relentle* some well-known stories of the New reader will go away with a much bette stand-ing of his purposes after reading this book.

Benjamin S. Carson, Sr., M.D., Professor and director of pediatric neurosurgery, The Johns Hopkins Medical Institutions

"As someone blest to know the author, Cecil Murphey, I encourage you to indulge in the spiritual depth of his book *The Relentless God*. With his gift of rich storytelling, Cec intricately weaves the Scripture throughout the pages of his compelling message of a God who accepts each one of us . . . flaws and all—never giving up on us!"

Susan Wales, Author and producer of *A Match Made in Heaven*

"A book of intense comfort for those of us who sometimes rationalize that perhaps God just 'gets' us and then moves on to chase someone else. Also reassuring are the author's vignettes—such as having the Holy Spirit speak words of life-changing encouragement directly to him while stand-ing impatiently in line at the dry cleaners."

Marion Bond West, Contributing editor/author, *Guideposts*

"In his easy, accessible style, Cec Murphey opens wide a window to the heart of God. We can feel the 'touch of the Holy' in these pages and know we truly have a God who will never let us go."

James Scott Bell, Co-author of THE SHANNON SAGA series

"So candid. No veneer. That's Cec Murphey's *The Relentless God*, a frank portrait of a believer grappling with the easy and brutal faces of faith. It takes the honesty of a Cecil Murphey to speak so freely and write so well."

Michael R. Smith, Author of *The Jesus Newspaper*, associate professor, Regent University's Washington Graduate Journalism Center

"Cec Murphey has impacted me since 1974 when I first met him as a student at Beulah Heights Bible College in Atlanta, Georgia. Over all these years *who* Cec is has overshadowed *what* Cec writes. In *The Relentless God*, Cec once more leads us in his own tranparent way. The power of this book lies in the way it makes the reader say, 'That's exactly how I feel.' It also frees the reader to deal with intense internal questions by finding freedom to ask them. Thank you, Cec, for paving the way for refreshing honesty."

Dr. Samuel Chand, President, Beulah Heights Bible College

"If you need encouragement to know that God loves you and desires fresh intimacy wih you, this book is a must. You will be recharged, refreshed, and renewed. Cecil Murphey helps you see that God will not let go of you!"

Gregory L. Jantz, Ph.D., Executive director, The Center for Counseling & Health Resources, Inc.

"A personal and provocative look at how God ceaselessly pursues and conforms his children into the likeness of Jesus Christ."

Bill Myers, Author of *The Face of God*

"As I read *The Relentless God*, by Cecil Murphey, several times I caught myself entering into prayer, talking with God about the issues the author deals with in such self-probing honesty. It was as though The-One-Who-Finds-Us, the Divine Pursuer, the Holy Invader reached out through these pages to nudge me, as he did the people in these stories."

Janet Chester Bly, Author of *Hope Lives Here*

"Cecil Murphey has a wonderful way with words . . . and in this, his newest book, he delights us with accounts of a relentless God who will not let go in his pursuit of each of us. A God who mounts "divine invasions" into the lives of ordinary people . . . people like you . . . people like me. A most encouraging message by a master writer!"

Nick Harrison, Author of *Magnificent Prayer*

The Relentless GOD

ENCOUNTERING THE ONE WHO WON'T LET GO

CECIL MURPHEY

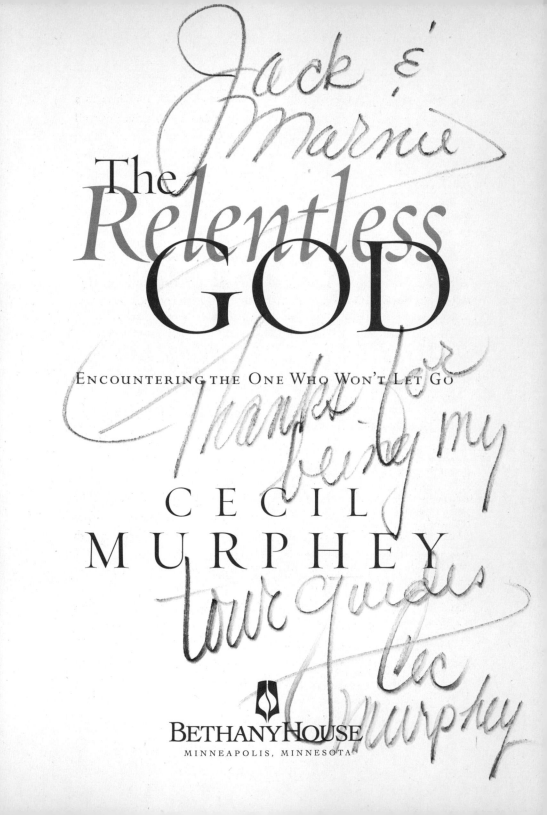

BETHANY HOUSE
MINNEAPOLIS, MINNESOTA

Jack & Marnie

Thanks for being my tour guides

Cec Murphey

Published by Bethany House Publishers
11400 Hampshire Avenue South
Bloomington, Minnesota 55438
www.bethanyhouse.com

Bethany House Publishers is a Division of
Baker Book House Company, Grand Rapids, Michigan

Printed in the United States of America by
Bethany Press International, Bloomington, Minnesota 55438

Library of Congress Cataloging-in-Publication Data

Murphey, Cecil B.
    The relentless God : encountering the one who won't let go / by Cecil Murphey.
      p.   cm.
    ISBN 0-7642-2587-1 (pbk.)
    1. God—Love. 2. Christian life—Presbyterian authors. I. Title.

BT140 .M87   2003
231.7—dc21   2002152599

ACKNOWLEDGMENTS

I want to thank several people God has used in that holy pursuit in my life:

- Jon Ludtke, who did so much to shape my teen years, and even now he remains one of the kindest, most compassionate men I've ever known.

- My African friends, most of them now dead, who hugged and enabled me to see God's grace at work, especially: Henry Nyakwana, Erastus Otieno, Nathaniel Jullo, Wilson Amwago, as well as AIM missionaries Maurice and Joan Wheatley.

- Members of the Bible Discovery Sunday school class. For the past eight years, you've thought I was doing all the teaching: Beth Wilson, Pat Fields, Bill and Vicky Rice, Dot Baker, Chuck and P. J. White, Cathy Patillo, Jeff and Joanna Tarrant, Maggie Yebra, Bradford Lakumi, Mary Hensley, Fred Turverey, Alice Brandt, Will and Tiv Alston, John and Teresa Day, Marc and Anna Melkerson,

Shirley Foster, Curtis and Louise Waites, Winn and Lynn Story, Mike Kaman, Cindy Brown, Bob and Betty Brown, Cille Harvey, Bill and Nancy Wren, Bob and Jenny Masterson, Susan and Steve Bearse, Maryalice Francisco, Keith Burke, Joyce Dorough, Bud and Cathy Purcell, Joyce Jacobs, Tim and Cathy Wilson, Judy Liedtke, Pat Dupuy, Christiana Holland, Kristen and Stan Stanfill, Byron and Jane Manderson, Don and Eleanor Reynolds, Cynthia and Jay Johnston, and Kathy Boyer.

- The other members of the "Gang of Four" for your friendship, challenges, and encouragement: Elaine Colvin, Wayne Holmes, and Simon Presland.
- My agent, Deidre Knight, still pushes me by saying, "You *do* have things to write."
- My editors Steven Laube and Christopher Soderstrom because you made my writing look even better.
- Special thanks and inexpressible love to my wife, Shirley, and my friend David Morgan.

Most of all, I'm grateful for the Relentless One who just won't give up on me.

Books by
CECIL MURPHEY
FROM BETHANY HOUSE PUBLISHERS

The God Who Pursues
The Relentless God

CECIL MURPHEY has authored or coauthored over eighty books. He has earned master's degrees in theology and education, taught school, mentored writers, and served as a missionary in Africa. He and his family live in Atlanta, Georgia. You may contact him at *www.CecilMurphey.com*.

CONTENTS

INTRODUCTION

S ome days I wish God would leave me alone. On those occasions, I'm tired of being "spiritual," weary with self-scrutiny, and discouraged over my lack of progress toward sainthood. Those are the days that make me wonder if my faith is any stronger or my commitment any holier than it was last year, or five years ago, or twenty. *Is it worth the effort?* I ask myself.

If God would ease up, I wouldn't have to think about obedience, holiness, commitment, surrender, and faithfulness. I wouldn't have to give much consideration to other people's feelings and needs. I could live like everyone else (or maybe it's only how I perceive other Christians live). "Why can't I be all right the way I am?" I ask. "Why does there always have to be *more?*"

Before I became a believer, I decided what I wanted to do and did it. After the Relentless Pursuer entered my life, the rules changed. God's invasion into my life brought in new standards and added complexity. Since then it's been more difficult to make choices. Now I need to pray for guidance. I'm pushed to examine the purity of my motives. That's rarely easy, and it's often impossible to admit to selfish desires or hidden agendas. No matter how much I want something, God still gets the veto vote over my decisions.

Yes, some days I wish God would leave me alone.

Obviously, those are my worst days. The rest of the time I'm thankful that I experience moments filled with excitement, contentment, and peace. A voice whispers, "My peace I give you." I sense strong arms embracing me and holding me tight. A warm hand lifts my face upward, and I can almost see God smiling down on me. Then I'm reminded: God loves me and wants only the best for me and won't allow me to settle for less. In short, God won't let me go.

Those are the best times and the occasions when I'm joyfully aware that I serve a relentless God—the One who refuses to let me just get by, be like anyone else, or be less than I can be.

Looking back to those early days as a believer, the turnaround in values and attitudes came as a major surprise to me. Not having come from a Christian background, my interest in God was spasmodic. Mostly it consisted of begging some Power, somewhere, when I wanted favors and ignoring anything religious when my life went well.

In my early twenties, however, a sudden and totally unexpected yearning for God filled my life. I hadn't been inside a church building for at least ten years, and I never thought about words such as *sin* or *salvation*. *Bible* and *prayer* weren't part of my vocabulary. Why, then, did I have a sudden hunger for meaning in my life when I wasn't even sure God existed?

At the time I was grieving over a broken love affair. Still, I have to ask, why then? Others had far worse experiences and weren't stirred to turn religious.

I have no way to answer that question. This much I know: It was the moment the Relentless One chose to invade my life. The divine intrusion could have come at any point or through many different situations. Perhaps that's why it was so powerful for me: God chose me, pursued me, and finally caught me.

Although I didn't use such words then, I knew I wouldn't be at peace with myself until I made my peace with God. I was aware of one thing: A deep desire to know and follow Jesus Christ controlled my life. Where did that yearning come from? At the time I had no idea; now I think I know.

The Holy Spirit had lassoed me long before, but the divine rope around my fleeing soul had finally reached its end. The One-Who-Won't-Let-Go stopped me; that tightening of the holy rope pulled my struggling soul backward. Although I believed I was free to do anything I chose, God had pursued me since childhood and hadn't let me get away. Since age eleven or twelve, when I dropped out of church, I thought I had outrun the divine chase, but I was wrong. The rope held.

Strangely enough, once I realized that the Divine Pursuer

had chased after me all those years, I stopped fighting. Perhaps a year later, when I read the Old Testament for the first time, I came upon a passage that enabled me to make sense of my experience. Speaking of non-Jews, it reads: "I was sought by those who did not ask for Me; I was found by those who did not seek Me" (Isaiah 65:1 NKJV).

When I read that verse, I accepted it as a way to explain the divine intervention in my life. This isn't to argue against the freedom of the human will. However, in recent decades we've put so much emphasis on what *we* do that we've obscured the other side of the picture: *God* is sovereign. That means God is in control and makes choices too. Isn't it time to emphasize once again what *God* does? Think of the divine encounter this way: It begins when the Holy Spirit invades our lives. Human sin created an impassable gulf between an imperfect humanity and a perfect divinity. No matter how hard we try, we can't earn or demand God's love. All good gifts come to us because the Creator-Savior comes into the sinful human world. God reaches down because we can't reach up high enough to make the connection. We call that *grace*.

Even though I can't explain grace, I'm content to say, "God caught me."

R

Once caught—once aware of this implanted divine hunger—I changed. I call it "implanted divine hunger" because that's the only way my own conversion makes sense to me. I had not gone looking for anything spiritual; none of my friends were believers; I didn't go to a church or drunkenly stumble into an evangelistic service; I hadn't opened a Bible since childhood. The Relentless One had stalked my path and in some unexplainable, mystical way had implanted a craving in my life for spiritual things. That was my beginning in the Christian faith—and it started with a thirst that would not be satisfied until I surrendered to Jesus Christ.

Despite occasional grumblings, I still yearn for more of the divine control in my life. Through the years since my conversion I've read the books, heard the sermons, gone to the seminars, and practiced what the experts told me. They have helped, but none of them satisfied me for long. I still hunger for more. Early in my Christian experience I set aside daily prayer times and faithfully read my Bible. I've done all the things I'd learned I was supposed to do.

Yet the hunger persisted.

"What more can I do?" is one way I've prayed. "Help me understand" is another. Gradually I grasped a powerful truth—we finally come to an end of our resources. We can only go so far in our yearning and our searching. At some point in our spiritual journey the Holy Spirit has to intervene, and not just once more but repeatedly and at many places along the way. I don't understand, but I accept the reality that the Sovereign One chooses how and when to break into our lives.

In an earlier book, *The God Who Pursues*,[1] I wrote about God shattering our protective walls without our consciously inviting it. I pointed out that the Holy One disrupts well-ordered lives, and we're never the same again. These times aren't always catastrophes or tragedies; they are "invasions from on high"—secret, sometimes silent, always internal, heavenly visitations. Afterward we can see ourselves more fully, perceive God more realistically, and grasp our situations with new insight. We rarely welcome such invasions. We may experience joy in the process, but that's definitely not our first emotional reaction.

In trying to explain these intrusions from the God-Who-Pursues-Us and who ultimately becomes the God-Who-Finds-Us, I start with three words: *God is holy*. In the Bible, "holy" means totally different, separated, and set apart for sacred use. In practical terms, it means the Holy—the One who is completely other than human—tears the heavens apart, taps us on the shoulder, and whispers, "This is what I want you to see about yourself."

The apostle Peter writes to early Christians, "Like obedient children, do not be conformed to the desires that you formerly had in ignorance. Instead, as [God] who called you is holy, be holy yourselves in all your conduct; for it is written, 'You shall be holy, for I am holy'" (1 Peter 1:14–16).

Most of us acknowledge that God keeps working in us, purifying us, seeking to make us holy (or, to use the older term, *sanctified*) so that we become more like Jesus Christ, the Perfect One. Nevertheless, we don't like getting too specific about the means and methods. Yahweh (or Jehovah) commands us to be holy, but too often we've assumed that holiness refs to adding more activity to our already-stressed lives. If we pray more, serve more, give more, or add more charitable service, we might make ourselves good enough, or so we think.

So how can we become holy like God? The answer is both simple and obvious. *We can't*. We move in the right direction only when the Spirit invades our lives and forces us to recognize our lack of wholeness (or holiness).

In the chapters that follow, I start with a divine invasion, where I saw my true self and shuddered with shock, denial, and shame. From there, I examine the lives of people in the New Testament, and, although our situations are different, God's purpose remains the same: "You shall be holy, for I the LORD your God am holy" (Leviticus 19:2).

These are divine invasions, and they come to change us, to make us more like the Holy One. Each such intrusion gives us the opportunity to ponder these words: "We know that all things work together for good for those who love God, who are called according to [God's] purpose . . . *to be conformed to the image of {God's} Son*" (Romans 8:28–29, emphasis mine).

May each of us take pleasure in the divine pursuit and rejoice that God cares so much—the divine hand never lets go.

Even more, we can remind ourselves that the Relentless

One will whisper, nudge, push, kick, shout, or simply make us miserable when we refuse to move forward. This is the Spirit who truly does things for our own good. This is the real picture of the God-Who-Won't-Release-Us.

CHAPTER ONE

REVEALING MY SECRETS

The words certainly didn't describe me. No one else—at least to my face—had ever used such descriptions. "No, they can't be true," I said again.

Then why did I feel so miserable? If what I had read wasn't accurate, why did the description disturb me? The inability to push aside what I heard as an accusation wouldn't go away. If true, those words depicted someone named Cec Murphey that I didn't know—*and someone I didn't like very much.*

This experience began when my best friend, David Morgan, talked with me about the Enneagram. I had known about it previously and had listened to a series of tapes by a Franciscan priest named Richard Rohr. The Enneagram is a personality theory that some Christians date back to early monastic movements. *Enneagram* means *nine,* and the system looks at all personalities in view of nine possibilities.

Parenthetically, I want to make it clear that I'm not endorsing the Enneagram or any other personality theory as *the* way to a closer walk with God. This is my story of the Holy breaking into my life and forcing me to look at myself.

Years earlier I had studied the Myers-Briggs Type Indicator and received delightful affirmation and encouragement. The Enneagram, however, while affirming positive characteristics, strips away the nice, encouraging descriptions about each of the personality types and goes on to push people to see their weaknesses.

When I read the description of my friend David, I nodded sagely and said, "This has nailed you." When I read the characteristics of another friend, I smiled at the accuracy it afforded. However, when I read my own profile in Rohr's book, immediately I recoiled. *This can't be,* I thought. The next day at the library I skimmed three different books that explained the Enneagram system and carefully read their descriptions of number two, which was supposed to reveal myself to me. I didn't like what I read.

That's when the Divine Pursuer wrapped holy arms around me and wouldn't let me go. I fought desperately, trying earnestly not to accept the startling portrait of myself. Nevertheless, the Holy held tight, and I couldn't run away.

The description cast me into despair because it said my root sin was *pride*. When I read those words the first time, I laughed. "Me? Proud?" One of the books spoke about it being a subtle sin, and number twos are puffed up but rarely seem aware. All three books and the tape series differed in some ways, but all unanimously gave the picture. "If this is accurate," I finally admitted, "here are some of the things I have to face about Cec Murphey."

If this is accurate? Didn't the tugging resistance in my heart and the tenacious denial in my mind tell me something? I've learned—through many divine interventions—that when I react strongly to anything, it's a fairly accurate statement about me. Okay, okay, so maybe it was a picture of me . . . but I didn't like the truth I tried to accept.

I learned that, like other number twos, I'm a people person. I like being around others and helping those in trouble. If anyone seeks a listening ear, a caring heart, or strong arms for an embrace, just call on me. That doesn't sound like sin, does it?

The description only gets started with those words. The reality of sin comes when I deny my needs. If I can absorb myself in helping someone else, the experts say, I avoid facing my own inadequacies and failures. I'm the "faithful friend," and that's been a source of pride in me, even though I wouldn't have called it pride.

"I can always count on you," friends have said for as long as I can remember. "No matter how bad things get in my life, I know you're there if I call." Yes, that was Cec—the confidant, the caregiver, the listener, and the loyal friend.

This sounds noble and exemplary, but the truth is that I *had* to be needed by others. I *depended* on expressions of appreciation, affirmation, and affection for my validation and sense of well-being. When I felt indispensable, I felt loved, and that covered up a lot of inner emptiness.

Another problem with number twos is that we're suscep-tible to flattery. "It seduces me every time," I finally admitted. Someone only had to say, "You never let me down" or "You're the one person I can turn to," and those words hooked me. I was blinded into believing that gaining approval was obtain-ing love and becoming more worthwhile.

"If there's one true Christian in the universe, I know it's you," was typical of the way one man began almost every tele-phone conversation. Within minutes, he had manipulated me so that I could give him whatever he wanted. It took me fif-teen years before I realized the seductiveness of his words.

The most awful part about being a number two is that I didn't seem to have needs. Deep within, I tried to avoid self-ishness; I gave unreservedly to others and served God faith-fully. I was willing to burn out for Jesus and couldn't say no to anyone who asked for help. Because I denied I had my own needs, I constantly volunteered, frequently took on tasks I regretted, and never considered questioning anyone in trouble.

I even had a Bible verse that I often quoted to myself: "How does God's love abide in anyone who has the world's goods and sees a brother or sister in need and yet refuses help?" (1 John 3:17).

I hated to admit it, but after an intense struggle over fac-ing the description of a number two, I finally cried out, "Yes, God, that is me! Pride is my sin." Instead of peace filling me, the acknowledgment evoked a dreadful sense of shame.

As I examined myself, I realized that ever since childhood,

whenever I felt needy, condemnation encircled me. I had made my own way in a chaotic family of codependents and alcoholics. Growing up, too often I had functioned as my mother's confidant and caregiver. I was the one who forced my two younger brothers to behave, and the more successfully I kept them in line, the more approval I received. It was an unconscious thing, but the reasoning must have been that the more I did for others, the fewer needs I had.

Almost immediately after my acceptance of being a number two, I heard myself say, "If I were a better Christian, I wouldn't be so inadequate." Those printed words (and the Holy Spirit holding my eyes to the page) forced me to say, "No, I am a needy person. Because I can now admit it, I am already becoming a better Christian." (This wasn't a spontaneous experience, because at least a day passed before I understood that last part.)

Studying the Enneagram also forced me to acknowledge my motives in charity. I loved giving and doing for others, but I had to be appreciated and approved in the process. If I wasn't affirmed for my noble gestures, I sometimes turned petty, petulant, and mean-spirited: "After all I've done for her . . ." or "So that's the thanks I get."

Until God opened my eyes through the Enneagram, my response was absolute and categorical denial: I couldn't embrace that this was truly me. For a couple of days after my initial awareness, I still struggled to realize that I had seen myself. "*Sometimes* I'm like that," I grudgingly admitted. It's difficult to face those parts of myself that I don't like, but the

Relentless One didn't give up. I don't remember how long it took, but I think it was two days before I finally said, "Okay, okay, that's a description of me."

When at last I surrendered, it was as if I looked into a mirror with a thousand-watt bulb over it. Every blemish and crease showed, and I recoiled at what I saw. As I pondered this vision, I was in a state of shock. "Is that really me? Surely I'm not that bad—am I?" I muttered to myself again and again. No matter how much I tried to deny it, I knew the answer.

My experience made me think of Adam and Eve in the Garden of Eden, and I had an inkling of shared identity with their shame. They had walked around for a long time, totally naked. But once they sinned—the Bible says that's when their eyes were opened—they knew their nakedness. For the first time they knew they had always been naked; previously, they'd had no awareness of not wearing clothes, and when they understood, they felt ashamed. The only way they knew to hide their nakedness—and their vulnerability—was to make clothes out of fig leaves and jump behind the bushes when God came along.

I had read their story before, but I'd never identified with the couple. However, now that God's silence had pushed me into looking at my "shadow side," I saw things I didn't really want to see. This is what we come up against when we struggle with such self-revelations: We concede our sinfulness and wail, "Help me! Show me what I need to know!"

When we feel intense pain at these moments of self-awareness, we cry out—or at least I did. "Where are your tender mercies? Where is the manifestation of loving-kindness? You hit me with overwhelming guilt and deep inner torment. Instead of affirmation and praise, you shine the spotlight on my nakedness and, like my ancestors, I feel thoroughly ashamed. Why do you do this to me?"

God didn't answer. But then, I didn't expect a reply; I only wanted peace. Instead, a heavy cloak of depression covered me. For perhaps forty-eight hours, I walked around numbly and did my work mechanically. My mind refused to turn away from what I had seen. *How can I live with myself if this is true?* I asked. *What if others see my secrets while I don't? Do people actually know those terrible things about me that I haven't known myself?* Unfortunately for me, I knew the answer was yes.

I felt naked, empty, and very, very needy. I picked up an old Bible and found a file card on which I had copied a quotation by the Puritan John Flavel (1630–1691). I had stuck the card inside my Bible and hadn't read it for at least five years. It expresses my experience: "When God intends to fill a soul, he first makes it empty. When he intends to enrich a soul, he first makes it poor. When he intends to exalt a soul, he first makes it sensible to its own miseries, wants, and nothingness."

I closed my old Bible, angry over the words I had read. At that moment it brought no solace or encouragement, and I could feel only pain and anguish. For a long time I'd carried around a particular image of myself: I was a committed Christian, a nice person who cared about people and who willingly helped others. In fact, this is true—I do care and I'm willing to go out of my way to help. Years ago my friend Doug Wilhite called me a cheerleader for others: "You lead the parade, and you keep looking over your shoulder and saying, 'Come on, you can do it. You can do it!' "

I liked hearing such words. I've mentored a number of people, especially other writers in whom I see talent. They've told both others and me how helpful I've been. How do I react? *Proud* is the true answer.

Did I acknowledge this pride? Of course not: I deflected the compliments, brushed them away, and even laughed at the idea that I could be conceited. But inwardly—*secretly*—I glowed with hubris.

⁕

These words have been difficult for me to write, especially when I pause and read them back to myself. They're tough to acknowledge because pride is one thing I've never associated with myself. My friends have called me kind, gentle, warm, and caring. Folks who don't like me have called me stubborn, angry, and mean. But *no one,* to my recollection, had ever called me proud.

My problem—which I see only in retrospect—is that I had developed my self-deception skills so well I couldn't sense pride at work in my life. Once I admitted to myself that "some" of this might be true, I earnestly prayed for God to show me the truth about myself. I knew it was a dangerous request to make of the God-Who-Relentlessly-Pursues-Us.

Like a shock to my brain, I heard the word *pride* from deep within. It was true, and the Holy wasn't going to let me run away. The tears came. I cringed the way King David must have cowered when Nathan the prophet accused him: "You are the man!" (2 Samuel 12:7 NKJV). He went on to ask, "Why have you despised the commandment of the LORD, to do evil in [God's] sight?" (12:9).

A thundering silence from within cut me sharply. For several hours the shame remained intense. During that time I asked myself several questions again and again. *What makes this so shameful? Why is pride such a big sin for me? What is it about facing the reality of pride that tortures me in ways that knowing about other sins doesn't?*

A few days later I was able to talk to David Morgan and tell him about the woundedness I was enduring. He hugged me and then talked to me in a way that made me know he understood. He said something like, "Cec, you have this image of yourself. It's not who you really are. It's more like some ideal self you keep trying to live up to. You've encased it in a suit of protective armor. Whenever a spear breaks through that armor, you feel the pain. To get over this, you have to face that you're not who you have idealized yourself to be."

I wanted to know the truth about myself, but I didn't want it to hurt. After my talk with David, a new thought came to me. I heard my own voice say, "Heavenly Father, you already know all this about me. You've known it all along.

You've seen my pride and all the other secret sins, *and you've loved me anyway.*"

As I spoke these words aloud, the shame lifted. A quiet peace came over me, followed by a deep sense of joy. It was going to be all right. The inflicted pain was part of the healing.

The Spirit's work had been accomplished. I saw myself through the eyes of the loving God. The Enneagram was the tool, although God could have used anything to enable me to see myself. I was now aware of the problem. It's a lifelong issue for me, and I know that despite it all, the Holy One has loved me enough to show me the truth about who I am.

CHAPTER TWO

WITHIN-THE-BOX GODLINESS

A week earlier Shirley, my wife, had gone in for a prenatal exam. "There may be some problems here," the doctor said. He spoke in quiet tones, but his words alerted us that this, our first baby, might not be healthy. He pointed out, as we knew, that Shirley also had a congenital heart condition.

In the meantime Shirley's mother had visited a small independent church where they regularly prayed for sick people, claiming that many of them received healing. She urged us to go and have Shirley prayed for. Although my wife was somewhat reluctant, we went. A man named Gus prayed for her, and Shirley knew she was healed. Three days later, when she returned to the doctor, he said she was doing absolutely fine; even her heart was normal.

In our excitement over Shirley's healing, we called our church and made an appointment to see our pastor so we could share our joy with him and with others.

"That is a cult, and you'd better not get involved with them!" was his first response to our story. He insisted that God does not heal today because we have well-trained doctors. In his mind, anyone who held meetings where they prayed for—and expected—physical healing had to belong to some kind of cultish organization and certainly couldn't be a Christian group.

His words shocked both of us. We had gone to him with great joy. Shirley felt physically stronger than she ever had in her life. She could even run up and down the stairs, something she had never been able to do before. Our not-yet-born baby was healthy.

For perhaps twenty minutes the words went back and forth. I had been a believer about a year, and he was the only pastor I had known. As I listened, I simply couldn't understand his objection. "They prayed for God's Holy Spirit to heal Shirley," I insisted. "Aren't the results enough?"

The evidence didn't matter; his mind was sealed tight. Before we left his office, he warned us about the dire consequences of listening to evil voices and being led astray.

Even more traumatic for us, Shirley and I had both been extremely active in our church; for instance, we regularly visited a local hospital where we sang and talked with the sick. Now we stopped being invited to go along. Suddenly they didn't need us for a number of activities we had participated in before. Doors didn't slam in our face; they closed gently. Shortly afterward, we left that church.

I tell this story because over the years I've thought a great deal about this pastor. Was he a godly man? Yes, I think so. Was he zealous for the Lord? Absolutely. Did he believe in Jesus Christ and adhere to all the orthodox tenets of the faith? I wouldn't question that for a second.

So what was the problem? My assessment is that he held to what I call "within-the-box godliness." That is, as long as it was a doctrine he had been clearly taught in his younger days or a matter of which our denomination approved, he supported it completely. Physical healing was not one of those teachings.

This isn't a crusade to support divine healing but rather an illustration of how I perceived our pastor. I learned a lot about the Bible under his ministry, and even today I read my Bible faithfully, a habit he helped me establish during my first year as a believer.

My term within-the-box godliness relates to good people, often the stalwarts of the church. If we look for faithfulness in service or want a volunteer, their names pop up quickly. It's just that they can't be coaxed outside the "established rules." They loyally tread the well-tramped paths; they recite the historical creeds; they are the most theologically trained. But they won't listen to unfamiliar thinking. Such ideas are outside the box and therefore unacceptable.

I'm not trying to categorize volunteers or the theologically astute; I'm simply trying to demonstrate a particular kind of mindset. When we look in the New Testament, we find an example: a priest named Zechariah. The introduction to the man speaks highly of him:

> In the days of King Herod of Judea, there was a priest named Zechariah, who belonged to the priestly order of Abijah. His wife was a descendant of Aaron, and her name was Elizabeth. Both of them were righteous before God, living blamelessly according to all the commandments and regulations of the Lord. But they had no children, because Elizabeth was barren, and both were getting on in years. (Luke 1:5–7)

In these three verses, Luke says nothing negative about Zechariah or Elizabeth: They are faithful servants of God; they keep all the commands of the law; they're exemplary believers. Zechariah is basically a good man, a priest who serves God just as he's supposed to. The only problem Luke mentions is that he and his wife are old and have never had children.

This account becomes the prelude to the story of Jesus' birth, and it starts with Zechariah's service. Every male from the tribe of Levi was automatically a priest. Although all of them served at the three major feasts of Passover, Pentecost, and Tabernacles, there were too many priests for everyday service. During his reign, King David solved the overpopulation problem by dividing the tribe of Levi into twenty-four different sections, each of which served twice a year for a period of one week. The clan of Abijah, of which Zechariah was a member, was eighth in rotation (1 Chronicles 24:6–19), and for many of the priests the highlight of each year revolved around those two weeks of duty. Within the terms of service for their order, they performed individual tasks decided by the drawing of lots.

Each morning and evening, inside the court of the priests, the officiating priest offered an animal sacrifice for the entire nation. Another burned incense, which is the duty Zechariah received by lot (as mentioned in Luke 1). Because of the large number of priests, some never had the opportunity to do these sacred tasks.

While one man burned incense inside the court of the priests, the people waited in the court of the Israelites. Tradition says that when the priest came into the holy place to offer incense, the people knew what he was doing because of the tinkling of a little bell, the sound of which signaled the time for them to pray. When the priest finished his task, he went to the rail between the two courts and blessed the people.

In this story, something happens that disrupts the ritualized activity: An angel stands at the right of the altar where Zechariah is to burn incense. Such a sight would probably have stunned anyone. Luke records that "when Zechariah saw him, he was terrified; and fear overwhelmed him" (1:12). As far as the Bible is concerned, not since the days of Malachi do we have a recorded instance of God speaking to the people of Israel, a silent period of about four hundred years. Consequently the appearance of something supernatural would have shaken up anyone.

The heavenly messenger standing before Zechariah isn't simply an apparition to scare him. As soon as the priest registers his terror, the angel says, "Do not be afraid, Zechariah, for your prayer has been heard. Your wife Elizabeth will bear you a son, and you will name him John. You will have joy and gladness, and many will rejoice at his birth" (1:13–14).

What an astounding experience! The old man is simply doing his duty, getting ready to burn incense as an offering to God, and a messenger of the Lord tells him not to be afraid: God has answered his prayer. We could assume that these words would be enough to reassure the man and maybe even make him break into a joyous shout, for the message is similar to the angelic appearance to the parents of Samson, and the words echo the promise to Abraham and Sarah. Zechariah, however, doesn't react with joy. He's both terrified and filled with doubt.

That's not even the end of the angel's message; he tells Zechariah a great deal about the son he will have, more than we find anywhere in the Bible about a promised child. The priest and his wife will name him John; "He will be great in the sight of the Lord" (1:15), and also a lifelong Nazirite:

> He must never drink wine or strong drink; even before his birth he will be filled with the Holy Spirit. He will turn many of the people of Israel to the Lord their God. With the spirit and power of Elijah he will go before him, to turn the hearts of parents to their children, and the disobedient to the wisdom of the righteous, to make ready a people prepared for the Lord. (Luke 1:15–17)

The word Nazirite means *separated*. This term usually refers to a vow individuals took to separate themselves temporarily from worldly concerns to consecrate themselves to God (as described in Numbers 6:1–8). Anyone could take the oath—male or female, servant or master, rich or poor. They didn't withdraw from society but continued their daily duties as they followed the strict requirements laid down in the Law of Moses. The Bible sets no time period, although Jewish tradition places thirty days as the usual length. Those taking the vow could choose to double or triple the period of commitment. Samson and Samuel were lifelong Nazirites, both of whose parents promised them to the Lord before their births. John, son of Zechariah, also called John the Baptist, would be the third such person mentioned in the Bible. God chose him.

The angel identifies himself as Gabriel; other than Michael, this is the only angel named in the Bible. Just telling the old man his name must have rung with significance: "I stand in the presence of God, and I have been sent to speak to you and to bring you this good news" (Luke 1:17).

In response, the priest asks, "How will I know that this is so? For I am an old man, and my wife is getting on in years" (1:18). Instead of a whoop of elation, Zechariah can't believe what's going on. Gabriel realizes this and adds, "Because you did not believe my words, which will be fulfilled in their time, you will become mute, unable to speak, until the day these things occur" (1:20).

Luke finishes the story by pointing his camera at the crowd, impatiently waiting for Zechariah to return. They knew approximately how long it took for a priest to burn incense in the curtained room, and they "wondered at his delay in the sanctuary. When he did come out, he could not speak to them, and they realized that he had seen a vision" (1:21–22).

This passage shows us the power of unbelief *in the godly*. Instead of rejoicing over the wonderful news that God had granted him a son in his old age, fear and doubt filled Zechariah's mind. As a well-instructed Jew, surely he knew about the miraculous births of Isaac, Samson, and Samuel.

Why the doubt? Was it because of within-the-box godliness? Since this wasn't the usual way for such things to take place, how could the angel's announcement be true? This account shows the Holy breaking into the priest's world, contradicting what he'd been taught all his life; he can't integrate this new information, even though Gabriel is the one who speaks it to him.

◊

As I think of this story, I'm reminded of an incident several years ago where an editor paired me with a high-profile Christian to co-write a book. As the man explained his theological position about the book of Revelation, he assumed I agreed. I didn't. I understood his viewpoint, for I had once believed the same thing.

"How could you have changed?" he demanded. "You still

believe in the Bible, don't you?"

"This doesn't have anything to do with the inspiration or accuracy of the Bible," I responded. "You have a theological theory. I don't agree with it."

"Theory? Theory? This is the truth!" He couldn't believe what he was hearing. When I challenged him to rethink his position, he said, "I was taught this forty years ago, and I have taught it all through my ministry. I do not intend to change now."

"Regardless of whether it's true?" I asked.

"I'm assured that my professors knew what they were talking about. That's good enough for me."

We did not do a book together.

Think what it would have meant for that prominent Christian to reexamine his viewpoint. If he had investigated and searched the Scriptures, he might have come out with a different interpretation. Then what? He would have to publicly retract his doctrinal pronouncements. It was easier to remain within the box of his tradition than to open his mind to alternative thinking.

❧

Zechariah portrays a within-the-box thinker: Regardless of what he sees and hears, nothing overcomes his doubt. The angelic appearance inside the court of the priests doesn't do it. When the angel tells him that God knows of his deep desire to have a son, apparently the old man's prayer for many years,

Zechariah still can't believe. Why? This is outside the norm.

The Holy is at work here. God sends an angel, and in most cases that's enough. It's enough for Mary and enough for Joseph, two uneducated peasants. It isn't enough, however, for the cultured Zechariah; he just knows this can't be true—nothing in his life has prepared him for such a moment. And thousands of years later, a prominent Christian leader gave the same response. Likewise, my first pastor's unbelief kept him from accepting a miracle.

In the case of Zechariah, the Holy steps in and says, "You will believe. You will be changed." For nine months Zechariah pays for his unbelief. Every day from the moment of Gabriel's appearance, the priest must have felt deep remorse for his lack of trust in the word of God's messenger. He must live within a box, but this time the box is silence. He can't hear; he can't speak. Perhaps the Holy longs to break down the sides of the box and expand his life.

For all those months the priest lives in that dreaded silence. Or maybe it becomes a blessed silence. Perhaps this becomes a period of immense joy. The message from the Holy was, "Accept it, and *then* you'll understand."

Instead, most of us insist on the reverse. "If you'll just help me understand, then I'll accept it." This is the attitude that doesn't want to risk and wants an easy journey of faith.

Is it possible that the work of the Relentless One is more than teaching us? Can it be that part of our growth means *unlearning*? We make assumptions, we accept others' views, and we absorb the values of those around us. (We don't like to admit this, but it's true.)

Another way to say this is that the longer we are in the Christian faith, the greater the tendency to hold a within-the-box form of godliness. We're quite sure we know how God thinks, plans, and acts. Our pastor could make no room in his theology for healing; a prominent leader couldn't conceive of an interpretation of Revelation different than the one he had learned forty years earlier. Zechariah couldn't grasp that the Creator could make him a father at his aged state in life.

I don't advocate an anything-goes theology. I'm firmly assured that the Bible is the infallible and inspired word of God. What I do advocate is that we keep open to new understandings or clearer ways to interpret what we're positive we've always understood. This isn't the place to show the changes in Christian theology over the past two thousand years, but some of it *has* changed. One example: The Protestant Reformation, with the newly understood concept that the just shall live by faith, shattered within-the-box thinking.

Theology changes; interpretations fluctuate. I'm reminded of a long-since-deceased Christian friend named Hans Dronen. When he was in his seventies, he said, "I think I know less about God now than I did fifty years ago." He was a man who refused within-the-box thinking but who remained open. The Relentless One pursued him, but I suspect in a more gentle, tender way, because Hans didn't seem to run in the wrong direction.

This makes me wonder. Does the Holy One laugh at our closed-mindedness?

Or maybe God only weeps.

CHAPTER THREE

How Can
This Be?

Although I had already entered my twenties, I served as a youth representative to a convocation of the World Council of Churches. The amount of theology I knew would have fit into a two-paragraph document. Fortunately for the council and for me, mine was a non-voting representation. I enjoyed the time, met a number of fine Christian leaders, and realized that I was only one of millions of believers in Jesus Christ from around the world.

One odd experience took place when I chatted with the pastor of a large congregation in California. He had a doctoral degree in theology and had written half a dozen volumes about the Christian faith. In our conversation, the matter of miracles came up.

"I just can't believe that Jesus walked on water," he said, "or that he literally provided food for at least five thousand people from a boy's lunch."

His words shocked me. I barely knew the stories he referred to, hadn't yet finished reading the Bible through once, and yet our attitudes about faith contrasted sharply. He knew the Bible well, but he didn't believe parts of it. I knew little of God's Word, but I believed all of it.

How can this be? I wondered. He's the one who should have believed much and encouraged my small faith. Instead, as we strolled along the shore of Lake Michigan, he asked me questions about faith. He'd shake his head and say, "I wish I could believe that easily."

&

As I ponder the first chapter of Luke's gospel, a similar situation exists. Zechariah was an elderly priest; by virtue of his office, he taught others and served God as a representative of the people. When the angel Gabriel appears to him, not only does fear grab him but also unbelief.

As Luke continues the story, the angel then goes to a peasant girl named Mary; she believes. She has questions, but she evinces no doubt about what God would do.

The account itself is rather simple. The angel appears to a young woman in the town of Nazareth, and assuming she followed the customs of her time, she would have been about thirteen or fourteen years old. Luke tells us she's engaged (or, in the older versions, *betrothed*) to a man named Joseph.

In our modern world we have no concept of the significance of betrothal. In Jewish culture, it lasted for a period of one year and was as binding on a couple as marriage; they could dissolve it only through divorce. If the man died during those months before the wedding, they referred to his beloved as "a widow who is a virgin."

Luke tells us that the angel suddenly appears to Mary because God sent him to her. Gabriel greets her, calls her "favored one," and adds, "The Lord is with you" (Luke 1:28).

> But she was much perplexed by his words and pondered what sort of greeting this might be. The angel said to her, "Do not be afraid, Mary, for you have found favor with God. And now, you will conceive in your womb and bear a son, and you will name him Jesus" (1:29–30).

The angel then says that Jesus will be great, will be called the Son of the Most High, and that he will receive the throne of his ancestor David.

These are powerful promises. Each Christmas we read and quickly pass over this story as if Mary were only one of a dozen women impregnated by the Holy Spirit. Instead, we need to marvel at this once-in-the-history-of-the-world event. That she was only a young teenager makes it even more amazing.

As a girl, Mary wouldn't have known the tenets of the Jewish faith. She probably knew the rules and followed the customs, but females rarely received any theological instruction. Further, this strange being appears in front of Mary and gives her an unheard-of message about what God is going to do. The Bible says she was perplexed. One translation reads, "confused and disturbed" (1:29 NLT).

Mary didn't say it couldn't happen; she didn't recoil in fear or try to run away. In fact, the story relates her asking only one question during the entire appearance of the angel: "How can this happen? I am not married!" (1:34 CEV).

"The Holy Spirit will come down to you, and God's power will come over you," answers Gabriel (1:35 CEV). He explains that Elizabeth, a relative of Mary and the wife of Zechariah, who was long known as barren, is now six months pregnant. This, I assume, is a way of explaining to Mary that God can break any natural law and do any kind of miracle. The angel's last recorded words are, "Nothing will be impossible with God" (1:37).

Why did God choose Mary? Nothing in the New Testament indicates anything special or outstanding about her. She was an ordinary teenager who lived in the town of Nazareth. We read nothing worthy of divine action or power.

Maybe that *is* a reason—God chooses an *unlikely* candidate. We find this all through the Bible: The Lord sometimes uses ignorant and/or insignificant people. We have Moses in the Old Testament and Paul in the New, but many of the individuals selected for God's higher purposes are ordinary people only God would designate.

Even more astounding is the example of Mary's faith. As I pointed out earlier, Zechariah should have been the one to affirm, "Yes, Lord, may it be as you say." Instead, the priest pulls back in doubt; the young woman believes the angel.

The most remarkable factor for me is her answer at the end of the encounter. She had already asked how it could be physically possible and receives an explanation that God will perform a miracle. She replies, "Here am I, the servant of the Lord; let it be with me according to your word" (1:38).

Mary understood, and her life exemplifies it. No matter how powerful the divine invasion of our lives, and no matter how mightily the Spirit uses any individual, it doesn't happen for our exaltation. Our answer is always to be, "Here am I, the servant of the Lord." We're only the flashlights that direct others to look heavenward. Additionally, Mary seems not to have taken advantage of her position as Jesus' mother. In all the gospel accounts she does nothing more outstanding than the other women. In fact, it's Mary Magdalene who takes burial spices to the tomb and who first sees Jesus after the Resurrection.

After Jesus' ascension, there is only one mention of His mother Mary. Luke lists the apostles who are praying in the Upper Room and adds, "They all joined together constantly in prayer, along with the women and Mary the mother of Jesus, and his brothers" (Acts 1:14 NIV).

If any woman in history had the right to say, "Look at me! I'm special!" it would be Mary. Instead, she and her other children take their place alongside Jesus' other disciples.

Perhaps one reason the Holy invaded the life of this young woman is that she not only completes the task of giving birth and believes the promises of God but she also remains who she is. Mary never exalts herself, even though others have built up a massive theology about her perfection and achievements.

Mary's life contrasts with many others. I've been around a number of celebrities—well-known entertainers, business leaders, and megastar preachers. People swarm around them, and they're constantly being told how wonderful and gifted they are. I haven't met one such person who hasn't been at least slightly tilted by the fanfare. Maybe in our culture it's impossible for popular people not to be tainted by the adulation of admirers around them.

"Here am I, the servant of the Lord" are the words of someone who has been found by the Holy Pursuer and rejoices in whatever path God chooses for her. Yet what would happen if each of us looked at our abilities (and we all have divinely given gifts) and asked, "How can this be?" How would we affect others if we recognized all our talents and insights as divinely given by the Holy Spirit and not something we earned or deserve?

If we perceived that the Relentless One was pursuing us even in the use of our abilities, what would that mean? Is it possible that part of the ongoing divine chase is not only to enable us to belong but also to serve? If so, it would mean that as we use our divinely given gifts we wouldn't focus on how clever, noble, or creative we are. Our exaltation wouldn't fill us with pride, because we would remain aware of the Source. Like Mary, we would accept ourselves only as instruments chosen for a task.

When we become *important,* we tend to act as if we're

doing special service or we're more highly committed if we give our divinely given abilities to serve others. What do we have that God didn't give us? If we win a promotion to office manager, have perfect pitch in one ear, or become known as the best cook in the community, doesn't that give us the opportunity to say, "Here am I, the servant of the Lord"?

To personalize this, I'm a writer. This is a gift I have received from God, and my task is to polish, to keep learning, and to improve this ability. I'm increasingly aware that I'm not famous for my writing and perhaps never will be. In fact, sometimes the idea of being famous frightens me. I'm scared because I've been around a number of celebrities—and I also mean *Christian* celebrities. I've been a ghostwriter for some of them and met others. Fame has a way of destroying, of tearing away, our dependence on God—of elevating and exalting us.

What would it have been like for Mary to walk through the streets of Nazareth or Jerusalem and have people bowing and falling at her feet? No matter how often she'd ask them not to, they'd do it anyway. Would it have changed her? Would she have begun to think of herself as special? Quite likely, because, again, fame has a way of seducing and inflating us. Any kind of exaltation or success tends to make us feel as if we have done everything by ourselves. God has helped, but we've done it.

Is it possible that the Relentless One continues to pursue us even in the midst of our role as first-rate administrator, top-grossing lawyer, talented surgeon, and award-winning writer? Can it be that divine pleasure in us comes not with our outstanding achievements but with our humility that says, "I have nothing and can never be anything except by God's grace"?

Maybe the most committed words we can affirm are these: "Here am I; the servant of the Lord. Let it be with me according to your word." Maybe that's when the Relentless One smiles and whispers, "At last! At last! You understand the pursuit."

CHAPTER FOUR

DEPART FROM ME

A man sees a miracle performed before his eyes and then freezes with terror: "Get out of here!" he screams to the wonder-worker.

I must have read this story at least five times before the impact of it struck me, because it didn't make a lot of sense. It seems to me that he should have cried out, "Abide with me!" instead of "Depart from me!"

This is a biblical account recorded in Luke 5:1–11. As Jesus stands beside Lake Gennesaret, also known as the Sea of Galilee, vast numbers of people crowd around him, eager to hear his teaching. Jesus spots two empty boats and gets into one that's owned by Simon Peter. He asks the fisherman to push out a little from the shore, and after Peter complies, Jesus sits and teaches.

When Jesus is finished speaking, he says to Simon, "Put

out into the deep water and let down your nets for a catch."
Simon answers,

> "Master, we have worked all night long but have
> caught nothing. Yet if you say so, I will let down the
> nets." When they had done this they caught so many fish
> that their nets were beginning to break. So they signaled
> their partners in the other boat to come and help them.
> And they came and filled both boats, so they began to
> sink. (Luke 5:4–7)

This is a powerful story of Jesus performing an unprece-
dented miracle. After a full night out on the lake, the professional catchers have returned with nothing but empty boats.
Now Jesus, a non-fisherman, tells them to once again throw
out their nets.

According to the text, Peter puts up only a mild resistance, but his words may have been a subtle rebuke, perhaps
an attempt to humor the teacher. Or maybe, in a kind of slow-
motion act of faith, Simon Peter is saying, "I'm not so sure
about this, but because *you* say so, I'll do it." Motives notwith-
standing, Peter and the others do exactly as Jesus asks. The
experts yield to the novice.

As I thought about this easy acquiescence, I realized that
in the previous chapter Luke records many miracles for which
Peter was likely present. For instance, at the synagogue in

Capernaum, Jesus heals a man whom the Bible describes as having "an unclean demon" (4:33)—some today would explain this as mental illness. The nature of the sickness may not be clear to modern readers, but the result leaves no doubt, because the man receives healing. Of the bystanders Luke says,

> They were all amazed and kept saying to one another, "What kind of utterance is this? For with authority and power he commands the unclean spirits, and out they come!" And a report about him began to reach every place in the region. (4:36–37)

Immediately following that incident, Jesus leaves the synagogue and goes to Peter's house. (The obvious assumption is that Peter was present in Capernaum before he takes Jesus to his home.) Peter's mother-in-law is ailing; Jesus sees the woman in bed with a high fever, touches her, and immediately she is healed.

The miracles aren't over yet. At sunset, while they're probably still at Peter's house, "all those who had any who were sick with various kinds of diseases brought them to him; and he laid his hands on each of them and cured them" (Luke 4:40).

The point I wish to make about the occurrences at the lakeside is that Peter has already observed the living power of Jesus: He knows that Jesus the teacher is also Jesus the miracle worker. When the Lord says, "Put out your nets and do it again," after the mild protest, Peter does exactly as he's told. His obedience pays off; they catch so many fish the load strains the nets. His companions have to bring the second boat over to help.

> They came and filled both boats, so that they began to sink. But when Simon Peter saw it, he fell down at Jesus' knees, saying, "Go away from me, Lord, for I am a sinful man." For he and all who were with him were amazed at the catch of fish that they had taken. (Luke 5:7–9)

Because miracle after miracle has taken place before Peter's eyes, it's easy to miss the significance of his reaction to the abundance of fish in the nets. Remember, these were professional fishermen who had been out all night and had returned with nothing. The catch of fish is supernatural; consequently, Peter quakes in amazement and calls himself a sinful man.

Why did he react in such a way? Why did he have a drastic response to the catch of fish?

Two things occur to me. First, this astounding event touches Peter personally. His mother-in-law had been seriously ill, but he was an observer, seeing it just like any other outsider. Now he directly benefits from an abundance of fish; the powerful Jesus touches *his* life.

Second, this is the Holy Intruder at work. This becomes that unforgettable moment when God breaks into Peter's life—unannounced, unexpected—and insight flashes into the man's soul.

This reaction could have happened at Capernaum when he saw the deranged man made well. When Jesus touched his mother-in-law, Peter could have fallen to his knees in awe and adoration. Instead, it happened at the Sea of Galilee, the place of Peter's employment.

The location or the circumstances aren't really important, but Peter's reaction to the event calls for our attention. Therapists, speaking about trauma in human life, usually say that events aren't as important as the way we react to them. For example, when a company downsizes and dismisses two hundred people, all receive pink slips, but how does each respond? Some collapse under the pressure and take it as personal rejection. Depression attacks others; they sit at home for weeks, bemoaning their fate. Others fight and refuse to be knocked down. Immediately they're out looking for new employment. A few of these will say, "This will lead me to an even better job."

Of the other fishermen present in the story—for certain James and John were there (Luke 5:10)—we read nothing of their reaction. Perhaps they are too busy pulling in the nets to reflect on anything else. Or maybe they did respond; however, this is Peter's occasion, and it is his reaction Luke highlights.

Peter has a great moment here, a necessary step toward his becoming the first of the apostles. Throughout the Gospels, he's constantly recognized as the leader of the other eleven. Is it possible that this is the first touch from the Holy to prepare Peter for such an important role?

I'll state it another way. Peter has followed Jesus for some time. He has been an eyewitness to feats of power and has listened to the vast wisdom of the Lord. In one sense this is just another incident like others he has seen. Miracles seem to take place every day in the company of Jesus.

What makes this one different? It's Peter's *insight*. This insight comes to him only from the Divine Intruder and makes this event stand out.

❦

Let's switch to a modern setting to show this principle at work. During the years I was a pastor in an Atlanta suburb, Jennie became a faithful member of our church. One evening she asked if she could say something to the entire congregation.

At age thirty-seven, Jennie had finally become a believer: "I went to church most of my life, but I never heard the Gospel preached. Then I came here to Riverdale Presbyterian Church, and finally I heard of God's love for me. I surrendered."

We smiled and listened as Jennie went on with her story, and we rejoiced with her as she explained the changes that had come into her life, into her children, and especially into her relationship with her still-unbelieving husband.

As I listened, I thought, *Yes, Jennie, that's wonderful. Unfortunately, your story isn't totally accurate.* I didn't correct her or devalue anything she said; she believed she had spoken the truth. She insisted—and I had heard her say it several times—that she had never heard the Gospel before she visited our church. However, I knew the Baptist church where Jennie had grown up. I also knew the longtime pastor of that church. If any servant of God had ever proclaimed the message of salvation, it was he.

The solution lies in the words *never heard*. In all those years Jennie attended that church, the Gospel had never penetrated her understanding. Thus she had not *heard*. Even so, because we don't grasp truth doesn't mean the words haven't been spoken; it simply means we haven't absorbed them. When the words or the meaning sink in, we're struck with amazement. We have suddenly recognized something that others may have perceived readily. I believe that's what happened to Peter. For the first time he *heard* (or felt or saw) the reality of Jesus Christ the Messiah.

This *never heard* concept works positively as well as negatively. For instance, a few months before writing this, in a conversation at church, someone referred to me as *gentle*. That word shocked me: I've seen myself as often brusque and extremely frank, so how could I be perceived as gentle? A few days later I received an e-mail from Alan Ross, a man with whom I was writing a book, and in it he said he appreciated my being gentle with him. Subsequently, a third incident occurred when an editor phoned me. He had a writing project he wanted me to consider but added, "I hesitate to offer this. You're such a gentle man, and he'll eat you alive if you're not careful, so I want you to know that I'll back you up."

Gentle? *Me?* Were they talking about the real me?

"Have I changed that much?" I asked my friend David Morgan. "I've been so harsh and thoughtless. . . ."

David laughed and reminded me of an incident, at least a decade earlier, when someone had used the same word of me. "But I guess you didn't hear it then," he said.

I stared back, still amazed. "How can this be? How could people have said such a word about me and I didn't *hear* it?"

"Gentle is only one way to describe you," he responded. "And you're not always gentle, but there is a kindness about you that people perceive and value."

When I approached Shirley about this, she gazed at me as if to inquire, "How can you ask that?"

I persisted: "This is something entirely new to me. Tell me. Help me define myself."

Shirley clasped my hand. "For as long as I've known you, you've tried to be gentle with other people's feelings." She leaned over and kissed my forehead.

Ah, now I heard the message. It had been true before, but the word meant nothing to me until I finally *heard* it.

∞

Peter's response is a moment of recognition, a time of awareness. He had always been depraved, but until that instant in his little boat he didn't recognize his sinfulness and Jesus' holiness. *Now* he saw the evil within his own heart.

Quite likely, until then, Peter had accepted himself as no better and no worse than anyone else.

The light shines on Peter, and he can't run away from what he has heard. He *is* a sinful man. I'm reasonably sure that Jesus, in his presence, had previously spoken about sin and the need to be forgiven. But Peter hadn't heard those words—at least not for himself. Finally, at a unique moment, right in the middle of a miracle, insight flashes. "Go away! I'm evil. I'm not worthy of being your follower." That's the essence of his words.

Luke doesn't record a direct response from Jesus. Instead, as Peter stares inward at all his wicked thoughts and deeds, Jesus points the fisherman beyond himself and assures, "Do not be afraid; from now on you will be catching people" (5:11).

This appears to be the first major step toward taming and molding Peter for his position of leadership. From other accounts, we know he's perceptive, quick-thinking, bold, and a natural leader. Is it possible that he might also be intolerant and unable to accept others who are less able? Could it be that the Holy first strikes him within and asks, "See this?" Once Peter recognizes himself as vile and sinful, he's ready for divine use. He's ready to fish for people and bring them to God.

It may well be that's the message for all of us. Until the divine light flashes within, we don't hear or grasp the messages that God persistently sends us. Then one day, seemingly in some ordinary context, the Holy breaks into our lives. We hear the truth for the first time. Sometimes it's so affirming we have difficulty accepting it; at other times, we don't like what we perceive as negative insight. The point of this decisive moment is that the Holy is at work, pushing us another step down the long road toward total commitment. This is how the One-Who-Finds-Us works in our lives.

CHAPTER FIVE

BREAKING THE RULES

Wilma (not her real name) sat across the desk from me and wept for what seemed an extremely long time. Her husband embraced her, but it didn't seem to help. Her body shook, and at one point her sobbing became hysterical.

I observed quietly, knowing that the anguish she'd held back for most of her twenty-four years was finally coming out. Now that she was feeling it, it hurt so much that she cried, "I can't take any more of this pain," still sobbing convulsively.

When Wilma could talk again, she told her husband and me much of what we had already known. Some of it could be traced to sibling rivalry, but the real issue was her parents. Until the birth of her younger brother when Wilma was ten, she had been the center of family life. From then on, she felt that her parents' hearts were large enough to embrace only one child, and she wasn't the one.

I understood Wilma's pain. On two occasions when I visited their home and her parents were there, I heard them speak to her with harsh demands that expected an immediate response, as if she were a thickheaded employee. With her brother, Harry, they spoke softly and kindly, as if they had been transformed into different people.

"Before I married, I followed all their rules," she said. "I never disobeyed them or stayed out late or did anything they disapproved of. Harry gets away with anything. He can stay out as late as he wants. He lies and they don't even question him." On and on the litany went. "I tried so hard. . . ." She wept again. "All my life I tried to please them, but I never did."

As I listened I thought of the famous passage we call the parable of the prodigal son, about a lad who wasted his inheritance and yet was embraced by his father.

A subtler story is that of Mary and Martha, the sisters of Lazarus: "A woman named Martha welcomed [Jesus] into her home. She had a sister named Mary, who sat at the Lord's feet and listened to what he was saying" (Luke 10:38–39).

Martha is playing the role of the hostess, probably by preparing food. In those days, to allow visitors to leave without being fed insulted them. Luke says only that she was distracted by her many tasks. And why wouldn't she be? They have a guest in their home, and custom said, by virtue of welcoming him inside, the family would do everything to make Jesus feel special. Martha keeps the rules; she does all the expected things.

But not Mary. She sits and listens, while her sister does all the work.

Finally an irritated Martha complains, "Lord, doesn't it bother you that my sister has left me to do all the work by myself? Tell her to come and help me!" (Luke 10:40 CEV).

That's a reasonable request. Yet even though Martha is doing all the right tasks of following the rules and obeying the customs, *she's* the one who gets rebuked by Jesus: "Martha, Martha! You are worried and upset about so many things, but only one thing is necessary. Mary has chosen what is best, and it will not be taken away from her" (10:41–42 CEV).

If I were female, I suspect I'd be like Martha and want to do everything to make my guest comfortable. I wouldn't be able to relax and pay attention. However, in effect, Jesus is saying to her, "It's all right, Martha. I don't want a fuss made over me. I'm on my way to Jerusalem to die. Forget the food and all the preparations you make for guests. Instead, sit quietly and listen. For now, that's the better thing."

For those of us who are the older-brother or older-sister types, this sounds like a stern rebuke. We try so hard to do everything right. We're the ones who guard the family honor, who finish every task we're assigned, and who work hard to win everyone's love. We're also the very ones who don't get the message! Instead, it's the undeserving ones who get the affection and attention. They break the rules and they get the blessings; we keep the rules and we get pushed aside.

That's one way to see these stories. That's certainly the way Wilma felt about life. Maybe Martha did too. The problem lies in *attitude*.

For many, keeping the rules is the way to get, to earn, and to deserve Jesus' blessings. Step outside the lines, and we dishonor God, or so we think. Yet all too often we discover that those who rush beyond the boundaries receive approval and affirmation. How can this be? If we live in a just world, why does it work that way?

❦

I want to think along this line by pointing to a different tale about rule keeping and rule breaking, the longest story in John's gospel. In chapter 4, Jesus and his disciples have left Judea and are heading north to Galilee, where most of them grew up. They pass through Samaria, taking the shortest route. (In those days, the land of Israel was only 120 miles from north to south, with three primary divisions of territory. Galilee lay in the extreme north, with Judea in the south and Samaria in between.) Through Samaria was the most direct way to Galilee and would have taken about three days on foot. If they took the alternate road, they would have to walk along the eastern side of the Jordan River and then re-cross it north of Samaria, which was far longer.

They decide to walk through Samaria and they reach Sychar at noon. Jesus is tired and hungry, so the disciples leave him and go into the city to buy food. I point out that even this was against the custom of the day. Jews considered Samaritans evil and called them dogs because they had intermarried with foreigners.

While Jesus sits by the well, a woman from the town comes to draw water. This immediately tells readers several things about her: They had wells inside the town, and for her to walk at least half a mile for water makes it appear that she's a social outcast, probably a prostitute. Also, if she had been one of the "good" people of the town, she would have waited and gone for water in the evening with the other women. Instead, she comes alone.

When Jesus asks her for a drink, the startled woman responds, "How is it that you, a Jew, ask a drink of me, a woman of Samaria?" (4:9). To make sure that readers grasp the significance, John adds this note: "Jews do not share things in common with Samaritans."

A lengthy dialogue takes place, much of it centering on Jesus speaking about spiritual things and the woman responding from a literal understanding of his words. For example, Jesus' first words read this way: "You don't know what God wants to give you, and you don't know who is asking you for a drink. If you did, you would ask me for the water that gives life" (4:10 CEV). She answers by noting that he doesn't have anything with which to draw water.

Their interaction, too voluminous to repeat here, continues, and it's obvious that she's slowly coming around to grasp what he's saying. Jesus then asks her to call her husband, and she says simply that she doesn't have one.

Jesus agrees and tells her that she has had five husbands and is now living with a man to whom she is not married. This is startling knowledge coming from Jesus, and she must have wondered how he knew this.

She admits that he is speaking the truth and then says, "Sir, I see that you are a prophet" (4:19). She goes on to what may appear at first to be a side issue—they are on Mount Gerizim, and she points out that for hundreds of years the Samaritans have worshiped there, while the Jews insist on worshiping at the temple in Jerusalem.

This may sound strange, but she's actually pushing the idea of keeping the rules. She makes this point: Our rule is to worship here at Mount Gerizim; your rule is to worship in Jerusalem.

Jesus finally cuts through everything; in effect, he says, "It's not about regulating worship. It's not whether you worship here or somewhere else. It's something more significant." He makes another statement, and this is where I perceive that the Holy invaded the woman:

> The hour is coming, and is now here, when the true worshipers will worship the Father in Spirit and in truth, for the Father seeks such as these to worship him. God is spirit, and those who worship him must worship in spirit and truth. (4:23–24)

The woman then makes one final statement: "I know that Messiah is coming (who is called Christ). When he comes, he will proclaim all things to us" (4:25).

Jesus responds with this stunning news: "I am he, the one who is speaking to you" (4:26).

&

We know the woman finally gets the message because she drops her water jar and races back to the village: "Come and see a man who told me everything I have ever done!" (4:29). The townspeople rush back with her, listen to Jesus, and many of them believe. Jesus stays with them two days:

> And many more believed because of his word. They said to the woman, "It is no longer because of what you said that we believe, for we have heard for ourselves, and we know that this is truly the Savior of the world" (4:41–42).

If this woman hadn't grasped that it was not keeping rules that brought God's favor and hadn't been aware that she was a most unlikely person for Jesus to talk to, she wouldn't have run back into Sychar. She had been the outcast, the despised woman, and now something has changed her. She met Jesus, he opens her heart, and she understands grace even if she doesn't know the word.

That's how the Holy operates. The rule keepers don't "hear" the message. I think it's because they can't hear; they're too heavily engaged in trying to do the right things, in making themselves better, or in "being good." Rule breakers aren't hung up there. They haven't been trying, or if they have, they haven't been succeeding. They may have been miserable in their waywardness, and one thing they surely realize—they need help.

The prodigal son knows he's worthless, and he's wasted his inheritance. His father's love—his extended hand—was the only thing that could save him. Mary ignores the rules by sitting and listening. She must have sensed that hearing Jesus was more important than feeding him.

Wilma's story, with which I began this chapter, didn't have a happy resolution at that time, and I don't know if it ever did. The last time I saw her, bitterness and anger still filled her heart. No matter what anyone said to her, she pointed to being treated unfairly for being good: "That's not the way things are supposed to be," she complained. But as long as we tightly grasp the boundaries, we'll keep on missing our encounter with the Holy.

Jesus tells the woman of Samaria that God is a spirit and that we must worship in spirit and in truth. "In spirit" means that life isn't about keeping rules, and it's certainly not about breaking rules either. The Holy is saying to us, "Our relationship turns in the right direction when you transcend regulations, slogans, patterns of behavior, or anything that holds you back from opening your hearts to me. It's not good behavior I seek but hungry hearts—receptive hearts like Mary's, thirsting hearts like the woman at the well."

When we try to earn anything from God by our behavior, we're missing it. The Holy breaks in to whisper, "I accept you exactly as you are right now." When we stop trying to be good enough or faithful enough, it says the Relentless Pursuer has caught us, embraces us, and is now ready to change our lives.

CHAPTER SIX

BEYOND WORDS

With a forged ID, my brother Mel began to race stock cars at age seventeen. He was five-foot-four, but he swaggered like a man a foot taller. Sensitive to any insult, he initiated the first blow, and if fights ensued, onlookers shamed his larger opponent. Another thing I remember is that he constantly proved that he could drink more than anyone else. In such ways, Mel screamed at the world that he was as good as (or better than) any other man.

I didn't know the term when I was younger, but it's often referred to as the short-man syndrome or the Napoleon complex. We live in a society that implies that real men are tall and physically strong; for some men, being short implies weakness or being somehow less than masculine. It doesn't help that they were teased about their size from childhood, taunted with nicknames such as Shorty or Half-Pint.

Sometimes such men forge ahead to prove their prowess as Melvin did.

Quite likely, Zacchaeus suffered from the Napoleon complex; the Bible says only that he was short of stature. Bad enough to have been taunted for physical lack, but people detested him because he was a chief tax collector in one of Israel's wealthiest and most important cities. Jericho was at the commercial crossroads and in a fertile area that grew dates and balsam and exported them throughout the Roman world.

The common people hated all tax collectors. First, of course, tax collectors worked for Rome, the oppressive government. Worse, they were usually dishonorable men and classified along with robbers and murderers. They weren't allowed to worship in the synagogues, which showed the depth of their social ostracism. Luke describes Zacchaeus as rich (19:2), and his use of this designation suggests a negative attitude toward the man, which he probably deserved.

Under the tax system, Rome assessed each district based on population and resources. The government officials sold tax rights to bidders, and as long as the collectors handed over the required funds at the end of each year, the Roman government didn't care how they gathered their funds or how much they extorted. In fact, the revenue agents, called "publicans" in some translations, retained whatever monies they collected over and above the assessments. Without the modern mass media to spread the word of the exact and official amount of taxation, unscrupulous individuals such as Zacchaeus discovered many opportunities to increase their personal wealth.

Here's a quick rundown of the system. It began with the poll tax—a tax people paid for living in the area. All males aged fourteen to sixty-five were to pay. Females also paid, but they began to pay when they reached twelve, the normal age of marriage. On top of that, there was a ground tax requiring them to give the government one-tenth of their grain and one-fifth of their oil or wine. Additionally, they paid an income tax of 1 percent.

That's not where the tax collectors made their income. Their profit—or extortion—came from what we call *duty*. Publicans could levy a duty on people just for using the main roads to transport goods. If they came by horse-drawn cart, the taxmen could assess each wheel of the vehicle as well as the animal pulling it. If farmers set up a stall in the public markets to sell their produce, they paid a tax. People like Zacchaeus often imposed a type of sales levy on items people purchased.

Scholars have recorded accounts of people being stopped on the roads by tax officials and being told to open their bundles or packages. The official could then impose a duty on the things he saw. If the owner didn't pay, the publican could confiscate the items or throw the poor person into jail.

With this background, we readily understand why everyone hated such officials. When Jesus decides to visit Jericho, and the chief tax assessor wants to get through to see him, it's obvious why no one will help Zacchaeus get a better view. The Bible says only that he wanted to see who Jesus was, and we probably ought not to make too much of this statement.

Although the short man may have wanted to see him for spiritual reasons, curiosity alone would have been enough.

I base this on my experiences of having lived six years in a rural section of Kenya. Whenever any dignitaries came through, people gathered and gawked. As foreigners, if we paused to buy oranges or bananas in a small town, we often had half a dozen locals trailing us—watching everything we did. In such a culture, for them to behave that way wasn't rude. "They are curious," one African said. "It is a compliment to you."

Whenever we missionaries went to the open marketplace and began to sing gospel songs, within minutes we had large crowds around us. Initially they would come and stare. When my wife began to play her accordion and Eunice Princic strummed her guitar, the crowds increased.

We always chose an open spot backed by trees so that we could have the people on three sides of us. Inevitably, children scampered up the trees behind us and perched in the large branches. That's how I envision this incident with Zacchaeus, who climbed into a sycamore.

Adults, even then, however, wouldn't naturally have done such an unbecoming thing: Climbing up trees was a child's activity, and it would have been beneath the dignity of a grown-up to sit on a sycamore limb. However, the chief tax collector probably had no dignity to protect. He certainly received no respect, and people wouldn't have shown him any courtesy. He had nothing to lose, and he was inquisitive.

Of course he would have heard of Jesus, because word

about healings and miracles had spread throughout the coun-
tryside. Quite likely, someone raced ahead to tell the villagers
that Jesus and his disciples were on the way. They hurriedly
leave their tasks and line the dirt road. They're curious, and
some of them probably want Jesus to heal them; they desire
to witness miracles. Zacchaeus is probably as wonder-filled as
anyone else.

What seems remarkable in this story is the way Jesus
behaves. He's on his way to Jerusalem and knows he's going
there to die. In the previous chapter, Jesus tells his disciples
for at least the third time that he's going to give up his life:

> Then he [Jesus] took the twelve aside and said to
> them, "See, we are going up to Jerusalem, and everything
> that is written about the Son of Man by the prophets will
> be accomplished. For he will be handed over to the Gen-
> tiles, and he will be mocked and insulted and spat upon.
> After they have flogged him, they will kill him, and on
> the third day he will rise again" (18:31–33).

Sounds rather clear, doesn't it? He's going to his death,
and he will be resurrected on the third day. But Luke adds,
"They understood nothing about all these things; in fact, what
he said was hidden from them, and they did not grasp what
was said" (18:34).

Let's try to imagine what this experience must be like for

Jesus. He's going to die and he knows it. We read in chapter 22 of his deep agony in the Garden, where he prays for God not to make him go through with this ordeal. This shows how heavily the future suffering must have weighed on Jesus. And yet in spite of all this, he's going forward and still ministering to the needs of others.

Luke 18 ends with the story of the healing of a blind beggar "as [Jesus] approached Jericho" (v. 35). Despite his own inner pain and the knowledge of what lies ahead, Jesus remains the ministering servant of God. To add to his unthinkable burden, the people he's closest to don't get the message. No matter how hard he tries to make it clear to them, their minds are filled with denial.

As Jesus approaches the tree where Zacchaeus sits in the branches, he calls the man by name. I don't make too much out of this fact. Surely the man had a reputation, and he was the *chief* tax collector. What I do find significant, however, is that Jesus stops and invites himself to stay at the man's house that day.

The taxman wouldn't have dared to extend the invitation himself. No one would stoop to talk to the despised servant of Rome, let alone share a meal with him. Jesus must have caused a stir as he calls the little man down from the tree and announces, "I'm going to spend time with you today."

In that simple invitation—those gracious words—the Holy operates. Jesus pauses and takes notice of the most rejected and despised man in the area. This is a person with whom nobody associates. Every decent, God-fearing Jew shuns him, but Jesus calls to him with love and compassion.

A change can now occur; this becomes the moment of the divine invasion for Zacchaeus. From Luke's account, we don't know if the rest of the story takes place beside the sycamore tree or if the two men go on to the house to eat. I like to think the latter because of the way Luke writes: "All who saw it began to grumble and said, 'He has gone to be the guest of one who is a sinner'" (Luke 19:7).

Custom dictated that Jesus not only go inside the home but that he eat a meal while present. As mentioned earlier, for the host not to feed a guest, no matter what the reason for the visit, would have insulted the person and shown an attitude of contempt.

Regardless of where it happens, Zacchaeus changes. At the end of the story, this man wants to make amends for his life. My wife figured out that if he fulfilled everything he promises to do, Zacchaeus would end up broke. In the Old Testament when people stole, they had to repay four times the amount. On top of that, if he gave away half of what he had left, it would leave him destitute. The amount of the repayment doesn't seem to trouble the man. Or he may simply have made an expansive gesture that meant "as much as possible"; he would make amends for his wrongdoing and not cheat anyone in the future.

Jesus applauds the tax collector's response, saying, "Today salvation has come to this house" (19:9), emphasizing the sincerity of the man's declaration.

We know the beginning of the story and we know the ending; we don't know much about the middle. That's where the mystery comes in—as it always does when the Holy touches a life. The Bible speaks so often about human need and God's intervening; we learn about sin and forgiveness, but in Scripture we learn almost nothing about what happens in conversion experiences.

Could it be that God doesn't want such information put in written form? Is it any wonder that when the saints of God write their own stories, they struggle to explain what happened to them? They can look backward to that life-changing point and then decry the inadequacy of words to express the experience itself.

If we had lengthy explanations, we can be sure that someone, somewhere, would come up with something like "Nine Steps to Conversion," and all converts would have to follow them slavishly. I can imagine a well-intentioned evangelist declaring by citing a biblical experience, "If you don't bow down, cry the words 'Forgive me' eight times, and then fall forward, you cannot become a child of God."

It is for good reason that this change is a mystery—an experience beyond words. Something happens to Zacchaeus, as it has happened to millions of others in the centuries since. In this account and all of the others I write about, the Holy invades, probes, confronts, and opens the understanding, but we find no formula for it. That's precisely the point!

The Holy Spirit intrudes into our lives, often at the most unexpected moment. When the Relentless One confronts us and makes us look into holy eyes, we change. Obviously some walk away unaltered from that moment of enlightenment, but here's a man who didn't.

To make this delightful story even more significant, Jesus bypasses the pious religious leaders in order to select *one* man—the most vilified person in Jericho—who has earned every bit of his unsavory reputation.

Jesus also targets the wealthiest man in Jericho. I'm sure that many of those who hated Zacchaeus also envied him, believing that the man had no worries or cares. "Money may not buy happiness," a cynic once said to me, "but it sure makes misery tolerable."

Or perhaps it was the reality of having more money than anyone else, or at least far more than most, that provides the wedge for the Holy to enter Zacchaeus's life.

As I thought of that possibility, I remember a pastor I knew twenty years ago named Bob MacMillan. He was in his thirties before he entered the ministry, and I heard from someone else that he had been a millionaire.

"That's true," he told me when I asked. "I had reached the top, and I had everything anyone could want." Then sadness lined his face as he added, "My success made me realize the emptiness of my life."

Was this Zacchaeus's story? He has ignored and shut his eyes to the derision and insults around him. He seeks wealth and possessions to insulate him from anger and hatred. He must have been a heartless man, because it took such qualities to reach the success level he enjoyed and to become the chief collector.

Then Jesus calls out to him and invites himself into the rich man's home. I wouldn't even begin to speculate on what goes on inside Zacchaeus when Jesus comes to Jericho. What is clear is that Jesus focuses on a needy soul and calls him by name.

Here's how I like to think of what happened. Jesus and Zacchaeus and the others go into the man's house. (It would have been rude not to invite the disciples inside as well.) As they sit and eat, Zacchaeus loses awareness of the others. He stares at Jesus, who says nothing.

In my version, it's the silence that touches Zacchaeus. He's been told for years that he's a scoundrel, a thief, a liar, and a robber. A new accusation won't bring any kind of change. But as he sits in a room where Jesus only stares into his eyes, the Holy can work.

I like to think Zacchaeus senses acceptance and compassion from Jesus. He feels that someone truly loves him for who he is and that grace shines through the Savior's eyes. The intangible, the nonverbal, often enables the Holy to penetrate a sinner's heart.

Here's my reason for this scenario. I haven't met many people whom I would label as holy, but I have met a few. In the presence of such people, words have little meaning. It's not what they say that makes a difference; it's who they are, and somehow their essence—their inner person—communicates in ways that go far beyond speech.

That's what I believe happened at Jericho that day. The notorious sinner experiences compassion, understanding, love, and acceptance. He knows without having to hear the right words. He knows because the Holy Spirit touches the human spirit. Zacchaeus becomes a new creature. It's an experience that's richer and more powerful than any words can describe.

The silence forces us to think and to look inward. The Holy Spirit uses such powerful ways to invade our lives to make us aware of our emptiness. Once aware of our neediness, the Pursuing One extends a helping hand. We know then that we're safe from all the harshness of life around us. We've been caught—and embraced—by the One who totally loves us. That makes the encounter worthwhile.

CHAPTER SEVEN

REVOLT AGAINST GRACE

At age sixteen I read *Les Misérables* for the first time. I didn't understand everything, so I skipped and skimmed along in the massive novel. Even so, that book profoundly impacted me. Thirty years later I read Victor Hugo's masterpiece again because I wanted to know if it would capture me in the same way. It still held up.

Since then I've read the complete book two more times, perused an inferior condensation, watched two movie versions, and attended the live musical performance. Each time I appreciated the story more.

What keeps me reading and responding to *Les Misérables*? I think it calls me back because it's a book about the human spirit and the power of divine grace. At sixteen I didn't understand grace or care about God, but I did understand injustice and tyranny. Jean Valjean became for me a model of a man who could change and help others change. The one significant part of the story I didn't comprehend until my second reading was the character and motivation of the villain, Inspector Javert.

Les Misérables centers on Jean Valjean, who went to jail for stealing bread to feed his sister's children. He tried to escape and ended up serving nineteen years in a brutal French prison. Released on parole, he is supposed to report to the authorities, which he never does. He receives shelter from a bishop when no one else will take him in. The parolee rewards that kindness by stealing silver that belongs to the bishop. When Valjean is captured and brought back by the gendarme, the bishop shockingly says to Valjean, "I gave you the candlesticks also, which are silver like the rest. . . . Why did you not take them along with your plates?"

In response to this gargantuan act of grace, Valjean is reformed and becomes a compassionate man who cares for the weak, the defenseless, and the hurting. In a particularly touching part of the story, he even adopts an orphan named Cosette.

Inspector Javert, however, hounds Valjean for twenty years. He discovers that Valjean has become M. Madeleine and has brought prosperity and dignity to a small town, even serving as their mayor. Despite Valjean's compassion, the police officer can only think of one thing—the law. For him, Valjean is a convict and must be punished, and most of *Les Misérables* hovers on his relentless pursuit. Each time Valjean moves (and no matter where he goes or what name he chooses, the former convict always lives an honorable life that helps others), Javert somehow finds and persecutes him.

Near the end of the book, students in Paris revolt, and they capture Javert. At great risk Jean Valjean rescues his enemy.

That's where the story causes my eyes to water each time I've read it. Javert knows the law; he understands guilt, justice, and punishment; he doesn't understand forgiveness or mercy. Most of all, he doesn't comprehend grace—it's beyond his capability to grasp.

A criminal (in his eyes) has saved his life. This catches Javert in a moral dilemma. Should he still pursue Valjean? Forget that he has sought him for two decades? Javert can do neither, and he resorts to the only solution open to him. He drowns himself in the Seine River.

For me that's the saddest part of *Les Misérables*. Javert can't accept grace—again, it's beyond his ability to understand. The man grasps duty, always performing it faithfully and diligently, but he doesn't realize anything that isn't bound up in the rigidity of law.

I bring this illustration to point to Judas Iscariot, the twelfth disciple of Jesus and the one who took his own life. The problem in explaining Judas is that Hollywood has produced a number of films in which they make Judas a hero or a visionary. The usual distortion is that he believed Jesus was the Messiah, and that by his betrayal, he tried to force Jesus to declare his destiny. Nice try, Hollywood, but it won't work.

A few have tried to cleanse the man's image by saying he became convinced that Jesus was a false messiah or that he was upset over Jesus' apparent indifference to the law, including his violation of the Sabbath and his constant association with the lower classes—the sinners.

Judas's name appears in three lists of the disciples, and always his is the last name given, along with the epitaph "the one who betrayed him [Jesus]." (See Matthew 10:4; Mark 3:19; Luke 6:16.)

The New Testament never speaks a favorable word about the man. In John 6, Jesus feeds the five thousand, then he preaches, and most of those who have followed him go away. Now he turns to his twelve disciples and asks if they, too, would leave him.

"Lord, to whom can we go? You have the words of eternal life" (6:68), answers Peter. He then adds a statement of his faith, "We have come to believe and know that you are the Holy One of God" (6:69).

Jesus' remarkably strong answer is, "Did I not choose you, the twelve? Yet one of you is a devil" (6:70). John then adds, "He was speaking of Judas son of Simon Iscariot, for he, though one of the twelve, was going to betray him" (6:71).

To me the most lasting picture of Judas in the New Testament occurs in John 12. Six days before Jesus' final Passover, all twelve disciples and the Master meet at the home of Lazarus. His sister Martha serves them food, and the action of Mary takes the spotlight. She "took a pound of costly perfume made of pure nard, anointed Jesus' feet and wiped them with her hair. The house was filled with the fragrance of the perfume" (12:3).

This is a lovely story, yet the reaction is where we get a glimpse of the true nature of Judas:

> But Judas Iscariot, one of his disciples (the one who was about to betray him), said, "Why was this perfume not sold for three hundred denarii [about a year's wages for a laborer] and the money given to the poor?" (John 12:4–5)

This might be a legitimate question to ask, and it has a practical ring to it, but John explains: "He said this not because he cared about the poor, but because he was a thief; he kept the common purse and used to steal what was put into it" (12:6). Jesus answered him, saying, " 'Leave her alone. She bought it so that she might keep it for the day of my burial' " (12:7).

Here we're made aware of Judas's unsavory character; in addition, John is preparing us for what happens next.

⁂

On Thursday evening the disciples meet in the Upper Room. Subsequently we read two significant statements about Judas.

First, "The devil had already put it into the heart of Judas son of Simon Iscariot to betray him" (John 13:2). Jesus obviously understood, but he made no mention of this fact.

Instead, during the supper the teacher began to wash the feet of the disciples. Although the gospel does not specifically say so, we assume he also washed Judas's feet; it would have been too obvious to the others if Jesus had ignored him or turned away from him. Jesus does say, "You are clean, though not all of you" (13:10). Again, an editorial comment by John reads, "For he knew who was to betray him; for this reason he said, 'Not all of you are clean' " (13:11). Then Jesus says that he has washed their feet as an example to them, that they should wash each others' feet—a way of self-humbling and serving— and goes on to once again predict his own death.

Second, Jesus "was troubled in spirit, and declared, 'Very truly, I tell you, one of you will betray me' " (13:21). The stunned disciples look around, and none of them seems to know the betrayer's identity. In fact, this turns into a time of self-reflection; finally Peter asks, "Lord, who is it?" (13:25).

We're not clear about the exact events, but Jesus declares that the betrayer will be the one to whom he hands bread. Scholars assume that Jesus holds out bread to all twelve, because they still don't know the guilty one. Finally, Jesus dips the bread into the dish and gives it to Judas. John makes an absolutely astounding statement: "After he [Judas] received the piece of bread, Satan entered into him. Jesus said to him, 'Do quickly what you are going to do' " (13:27).

The others have no idea what's going on. John says,

Some thought that, because Judas had the common purse, Jesus was telling him, "Buy what we need for the festival"; or, that he should give something to the poor. So, after receiving the piece of bread, he [Judas] immediately went out. And it was night. (13:29–30)

After this, Judas becomes the central character in the betrayal and arrest of Jesus. However,

> When Judas, his betrayer, saw that Jesus was condemned, he repented and brought back the thirty pieces of silver to the chief priests and the elders. He said, "I have sinned by betraying innocent blood." But they said, "What is that to us? See to it yourself" (Matthew 27:3–4).

Matthew tells us that Judas threw down the pieces of silver inside the temple and "he departed; and he went and hanged himself" (27:5). Luke also gives an account of his death, and we find a few more details of his suicide in the first chapter of Acts.

The Bible speaks little about intentions and motivations, so some of what we interpret must come from our understanding of what is not written. This much seems clear: A reading of all the verses about Judas certainly shows no justification for making him a good man. It makes no sense to think that Judas ever could have conceived of his selling out Jesus for any kind of honorable reason. He was a thief; he stole money. Betraying Jesus for thirty pieces of silver fits the man's character.

Now that I've stated all this, I want to explain why I've written about Judas as one who encountered and was pursued by the Holy.

My sense is that until Judas took the bread from the hand of Jesus at the Last Supper, he still had a choice. At that moment, the gospel writers tell us, Satan entered Judas. I take that to mean that the man had fully committed himself to carrying out the evil deed. From that moment there is no turning back.

Judas's encounter with the Holy comes at the moment of realization of what he has done: *He has betrayed Jesus.* He doesn't call him the Messiah, but he does call him an innocent man. As he stares at the silver coins in his hand, the thief realizes the enormity of his wrongdoing.

Here's my question: Could Judas have been forgiven? Matthew says he repented—and he shows his contrition by throwing down the money. But forgiven? That's where the problem lies.

The Holy has pursued the disciple and in the moment of self-revelation, Judas stares at himself. He realizes what he has done: He has betrayed the Savior; he has been an instrument of Satan. He has done the utmost evil deed.

Yet Judas has committed no unforgivable crime. He could cry out to God and receive divine forgiveness. My theology says that God's forgiveness is always there and held out to us, ready for us. Our responsibility is to touch the outstretched hand and receive.

That's what Judas can't bring himself to do. His actions

echo those of Cain, who cried out, "My punishment is greater than I can bear!" (Genesis 4:13). Judas sees himself as totally, utterly, irretrievably evil. Guilt and shame must have overwhelmed the man so deeply that he couldn't bear to stare in the mirror at his own reflection.

That's when suicide happens: when we feel hopeless, when we see no way out of our pain. When we'd rather die than live with ourselves.

Judas and Javert are similar: One follows the law and one breaks the law, and yet when they encounter grace, here's what they have in common: They can't receive it. They have nothing in themselves to allow them to receive kindness when they know they deserve punishment.

All twelve of the disciples fail Jesus. Except for John, all flee from the Savior in his final hour. Judas has gone beyond their acts of denial and fear, because he brings the Romans and priests to the garden. He leads them to Jesus.

How can that man possibly face Peter, James, Andrew, and the others again? Only by self-humbling and begging them to forgive him could this happen. Even more serious, how can he live with himself? Obviously, he can't.

This is the saddest kind of encounter with the Holy. It's a flawed thinking that says, "My sin is beyond God's grace, beyond divine love."

When the Holy chases and invades, the purpose is to make

us grasp the ugliness of our features, but it's also to extend grace. Judas grasped the first part of the message, but he couldn't accept the second. Taking his own life seemed the only answer.

◆

As I thought of the real Judas and the fictitious Javert, it made me remember a testimony I heard during my college days. The woman speaker—and I've forgotten her name—said that she and her husband had gone to Japan to serve several years before World War II. They were evacuated only days before the Japanese bombed Pearl Harbor.

About a decade earlier, she, her husband, and their two sons were holding open-air meetings in one of the major cities, proclaiming a loving, caring God. One enraged Japanese man confronted the older son, screaming at him to shut up. When he refused, the angry man knifed him, and he later died.

Once the family had found healing for their loss, the woman's husband went to the prison to see the young killer. She said he arrived just in time to prevent the convicted man from hanging himself. The father said, "You took my son's life. Now I want you to take his place." She said that they both pleaded with the authorities and got the young man released. In his gratitude and appreciation, he became a believer and a witness for Christ until he died during the Nagasaki bombing.

For me that true story illustrates how grace works. When we see ourselves with all our warts, scars, and spiritual disfigurement, God never turns away. Instead, God embraces us.

To further illustrate: When I was a pastor, a woman visited our church on a day we served the Lord's Supper. Ordinarily we had the bread and juice served to people as they sat in their pews, but on that occasion I asked everyone to come forward and take it from me. As she held the bread, her hand trembled.

"In Jesus Christ you are forgiven," I said. "If you believe this, then eat."

She hesitated, staring at me, and I repeated the words. She finally ate the bread and drank from the cup.

The next day she visited my office. "I went to church yesterday to give God one final chance," she stated. She told me of the mess she had made of her life—and it was quite an entangled array that included two divorces, abandoning the children from both marriages, a variety of sexual experiences, experimentation with drugs, a brief jail sentence, and then getting fired for not being able to do her job. "I was going to take my life," she said.

"What stopped you?" I asked.

She told me that as a child her grandmother had taken her to church and used to say, "Lay your burdens at the feet of Jesus, and he'll take care of you."

"I had done so many terrible things," she went on. "I didn't think God would forgive me. So I came here. I wanted to hear something from God or to feel God would give me another chance. When you said I was forgiven, it was like a jolt in my body. I knew, in a way that I couldn't understand how I knew, but I *was* forgiven."

That's the happier ending. She stared at herself, despised what she saw, but before she took her life, she was willing to give God one more chance.

One more chance is all God needs in any of our lives. This is the Relentless One who chases us through the dark paths of life, always pursuing, always reaching toward us to embrace us. This is the One who, on capturing us, whispers, "I love you with an everlasting love."

This is how the Divine Pursuer works and continues to work. No matter where we are in our spiritual lives or how badly we fail after we're Christians, grace never dries up. It always flows abundantly. The word of the Pursuer to us is always "Return. Return."

CHAPTER EIGHT

REWARDING DOUBTS

For most of my life my intent has been to *understand*. I've assumed that if I could understand a person, a theory, or a problem, I would be all right and I could handle every possible situation.

I once worked with a woman named Charlotte, who had the sharpest, most acidic tongue of anyone I had ever met. She smiled often in the midst of her harshness as if to deflect the impact; even so, her biting words cut deeply. I wasn't the only one wounded by her rapier responses. In fact, I didn't receive many of them, but my co-workers did regularly.

However, one day she attacked me. For perhaps two minutes her words tore me apart. As I walked out of the office, my hands were shaking, and I struggled not to explode with rage. There have been few times in my life when I've been that angry. Throughout the day and into the evening I went over and over the things she had said—as we tend to do when someone hurts us markedly.

I didn't sleep well that night, and my anger still surged the next morning. When Charlotte walked into the office, she greeted me the way she did every day. It amazed me that she acted no differently than she always had. That sameness inflamed my anger; she showed no shame or remorse.

At about ten-thirty that morning she made another pointed comment, and this time I was ready for her.

"I'll bet you stay up most nights trying to figure out how you can make the meanest comments. I have to hand it to you, Charlotte. You're mean to everyone. You hurt me yesterday, but I guess you're so used to knocking people around you don't even notice it! If anyone ever gave an award for being the meanest person in the state, you'd win the honor!"

Her eyes widened, and shock filled her face. She opened her mouth to speak but no words came out. Tears slowly slid down her cheeks as she stared at me.

"You don't know?" I asked. "You don't realize how much you hurt people?"

"Hurt? I was making a joke. I . . . I do that with everyone. I thought—I thought you knew I wasn't serious."

"How would I know that?" I refused to let her crying cause me to back down. "You tear down everyone." I went on a verbal rampage, giving her half a dozen examples.

Charlotte, still sitting at her desk, put her hands in front of her face and wept. "I . . . I didn't know—I didn't know I hurt anyone."

At lunchtime she apologized to me, and I forgave her. Then she told me about herself. When she had barely gotten into her teens, she discovered that by saying everything in a sharp, caustic tone, everyone thought she was funny, and no one took her seriously.

Charlotte was now in her mid-twenties, and she was still acting as if she were fourteen. What had been cute then was now harsh and cruel. "I didn't know . . . I didn't know," she kept saying.

Once I heard her story, my anger evaporated; I felt compassion. I understood her, and because I understood I could forgive.

That's how I've tended to operate my life. "To understand all is to forgive all," wrote Oscar Wilde. This had become one of my mottoes.

One of the reasons I spend time on this concept is that I think it fits Thomas the apostle. People like Thomas have to understand; once they understand, they can cope with what's going on. Such people need concrete, pragmatic explanation, and then they can act. For them, to understand is to accept. I want to show how this worked in Thomas's life and how that's the very area into which the Holy rushed for an encounter.

Thomas is chosen as one of the twelve disciples, but there is almost nothing recorded about him until John 11. There we read the story of Lazarus: He is extremely ill, and his sisters, Mary and Martha, send a message to the Lord. Jesus does not go.

Jesus' enemies are waiting for him and have been trying to find ways to destroy him. Finally Jesus tells his disciples that Lazarus is asleep; they misunderstand and think that Jesus means that the man has recovered. No, Jesus explains, Lazarus has died. Jesus is now going to Bethany to see him and to raise him from the dead.

This is where Thomas speaks up. He makes a bold statement—one that many people often fail to notice: "Let us also go, that we may die with him" (11:16).

Thomas *understands* the danger. He's well aware that the religious leaders want to stop Jesus from teaching and preaching. This isn't any secret, something going on only in dark places. In fact, the Jewish authorities can't arrest the Master because crowds follow him everywhere.

When Jesus decides to go to Bethany, Thomas seems to be the most clued in with regard to the consequences. Bethany is a small town just a few miles outside of Jerusalem. If Jesus goes to mourn the death of Lazarus, there won't be many people around. Jesus faces this distinct possibility: To go could mean his life. Thomas's response indicates that he believes it's more than a possibility; it's a certainty.

In that group of twelve faithful followers, who speaks up in support of Jesus? Just one man, and that's Thomas. Always the practical one, he understands exactly what this means. As far as Thomas is concerned, and his words seem accepted by the others if they go to Bethany with Jesus, they will face death.

"Let us also go, that we may die with him." Thomas, and only Thomas, openly faces that reality. These are not the words of a worried man; they come from a follower who knows, or at least assumes, that if he and others go with Jesus, they will all be killed.

These aren't the words of a doubter, as he's often called. These are the words of a person who knows what he can expect; he understands the gravity of the situation. He has processed the information, and his commitment to Jesus Christ enables him to say to the others, "I'm ready to die for him."

They do go with Jesus, and subsequently we read of the wonderful miracle of Lazarus's resurrection. The Jews don't entrap Jesus, but the tension is growing. Each step forward means a step closer to death.

As we fast-forward, the next scene with Thomas takes place in the Upper Room, where Jesus celebrates his final meal with his disciples. He's in the midst of giving them instructions; they still don't grasp that his life is going to be given away.

Jesus speaks the beloved words recorded in John 14. He urges them not to have troubled hearts but to believe, and says that he is leaving to prepare a place for them in one of the many dwelling places in his Father's house: I "will take you to myself, so that where I am, there you may be also. And you know the way to the place where I am going" (14:3–4).

We understand Jesus' references because we have looked at

this story from both sides of his death and resurrection. We know what he means, but they didn't. Thomas, aware only of the present, asks a sensible question: "Lord, we do not know where you are going. How can we know the way?" (13:5). It's as if he's saying, "I don't have the slightest idea what you mean. How can we be somewhere with you when we don't *understand* what you're talking about?"

Jesus answers again, just as cryptically: "I am the way, and the truth, and the life. No one comes to the Father except through me" (14:6).

Philip then takes the practical step, asking for Jesus to show them the Father. Jesus seems disappointed that after all they have seen and heard, they still don't grasp that he and the Father are the same. Although we read no additional details, we assume—and later events confirm—that they still don't comprehend.

This scene in the Upper Room takes place on Thursday, before Jesus goes to Gethsemane to pray. Later, when Judas brings the authorities to capture Jesus, Thomas runs away. He's not the only one, because all of them flee for their lives. None of them behaved bravely.

❧

We fast-forward once more to the evening following Jesus' resurrection. The Lord appears again to the disciples in the Upper Room; Thomas isn't there. Later, when he hears, ever the pragmatic one, Thomas doesn't accept the appearance of Jesus as being real.

The other disciples told him, "We have seen the Lord." But he said to them, "Unless I see the mark of the nails in his hands, and put . . . my hand in his side, I will not believe" (John 20:25).

This is where Christians have historically labeled him "doubting Thomas." That may be true, but his doubts are different from how we traditionally think. This is a man who has followed Jesus for three years, who has taken a bold stand to go with him to the home of Lazarus even in the face of death. Then, like everyone in Jerusalem, he learns that the Romans have crucified Jesus and that Joseph has buried him in a tomb. He hears of the Resurrection from the others, but this is something he's never known or heard of before—he has no experience with it. Even seeing the dead Lazarus resuscitated hasn't made this clear to him: "I just can't accept it" is his attitude.

If we push away from the concept of doubt, we can see something else at work. This is the man who can't embrace what he doesn't understand. It's the same man crying out, "If you'll just let me grasp all of this, I'll believe!"

How can a man who was crucified—who endured a slow, excruciating death—now be alive? How can a rational mind comprehend that fact? Of course, it's a statement of faith. Thomas, or anyone else, must *first* believe and *then* see. Thomas, however, like many of us today, operates on the principle of let-me-understand-and-then-I'll-believe.

A week later, all the disciples are together; Thomas is with them this time. Jesus walks into the room and greets them, and then he steps up to Thomas and says, "Put your finger here and see my hands. Reach out your hand and put it in my side. Do not doubt but believe" (20:27).

"My Lord and my God!" (20:28). Now Thomas believes.

This is the powerful moment. The Holy Pursuer touches him. As Jesus stands in front of him, Thomas obviously sees the marks left by the nails; he doesn't need to touch the body. He *knows*. No longer does Thomas need to understand first and then believe. Now the situation is reversed, as if he were to say, "I believe, and now I can understand."

Jesus then makes a significant statement to Thomas, one that echoes through the centuries: "Have you believed because you have seen me? Blessed are those who have not seen and yet have come to believe" (20:29).

Here is the life-altering encounter with the Holy. In that moment of actually seeing Jesus in front of him, Thomas believes in the Resurrection. His doubts and his need for understanding vanish. Until now, this is the man who asks for reasons, for explanations, for enough information that he can acknowledge reality. Finally, he sees Jesus alive, and that is enough.

❧

We who read these words centuries later grapple with the same issues: "God, just help me understand this," we pray. "If I could comprehend all of these things, I could believe them."

I think of my own search for God. I'd read a few chapters

in the New Testament, and I'd shake my head in confusion. "I just don't understand this," I'd say aloud. "It just doesn't make sense to me." The word *why* frequently came from my lips. *Why* did God do it that way? *Why* did Jesus have to die? *Why* would God let the death of one person who did nothing wrong take the place of countless millions who did everything wrong?

As I continued to read God's Word, talked to Christians, sat in Bible studies, and asked questions, I began to understand some of the basic teachings, but I still didn't find satisfactory answers to my difficult queries. Then one night I realized something had happened to me. Around midnight, after struggling over my inability to comprehend, I walked down a darkened street. Impulsively, I stopped in front of a tiny church. The front door was unlocked, so I went inside. One small overhead light gave enough illumination so that I didn't stumble over anything. I sat in a pew and bowed my head.

"I still don't understand all this," I heard myself say to God, "and yet . . . and yet I believe it." Then, aware of what I had just said, I shifted quickly. "How can I put my trust in it if I don't comprehend?" Because I persisted in believing that understanding comes first, I sat there confused. "How can this be?" I went on. "How can I put my faith in you and yet not understand most of the things written in the Bible?"

My situation wasn't all that different from that of Thomas. In that dark, quiet building, I faced a great crisis of my burgeoning faith and didn't know it. I would come back to this essential problem again and again. In the days ahead as I struggled to walk with God, certain things wouldn't make sense to me and the questions would erupt again. *Why would God do this? How could God let him get away with that? Why doesn't God answer my prayers? Why is such a godly person sick, while so many sinful people have no physical problems?*

It took me a long time to realize that as long as we insist on understanding as the first step, we won't ever figure it out. Instead, if we can turn around and say, "I believe," things change.

That night I sat in the church pew for a long time. Slowly I realized something for the first time in my life. I couldn't explain my rationale behind it, but somehow I knew: God loved me. It was an inner knowledge that hadn't come because someone had taught me or because I'd read about it in the Bible. It didn't come because I had gone through a reasoning process, with God's love for me being the conclusion.

I can't explain how I knew, only that I did. In some deep, unfathomable part of my inner being, the Holy Pursuer held me tight. Tears filled my eyes and a wave of embarrassment came over me. What was stirring my emotions? Was I caught up in some sentimental claptrap? Just then I pushed aside my thinking. I really didn't care about the reasons. To understand wasn't important.

I knew—with a certainty that defied explanation—that God loved me. Despite my lack of understanding, I was at peace.

Hours later I left that building aware that it was the first true inner peace I had experienced in my life. Questions buzzed inside my head, and I even laughed at myself. "I believe this, and I still can't explain it!"

At that moment I felt as Thomas must have when he cried out, "My Lord and my God!" No one could have taken that certainty from me. I didn't see nail-pierced hands, and no vision filled my eyes.

But I knew.

I wonder if this isn't a picture of Thomas. Three years before the Resurrection Jesus called him to follow, and he did. He kept asking questions, trying to figure out the message and the methods, but they never made sense. He built his hopes around the Messiah who would free them from Rome—which was the *understanding* of most faithful Jews of that time. Political overthrow never happened; the Victor became the victim, and he died. How could Thomas believe? Nothing made sense.

Then comes the touch of the Holy. Thomas finally sees the pierced hands and he still has no explanation. The logic isn't any clearer. Jesus explains nothing. But in that Upper Room, Thomas believes. The Holy Pursuer has gotten through to the disciple. Thomas's faith transcends his search for understanding.

Again, Jesus says to him, "Thomas, do you have faith because you have seen me? The people who have faith in me without seeing me are the ones who are really blessed!" (John 20:29 CEV). Once the Pursuer has touched Thomas, the man leaves behind his questions and his need for explanation.

That same Holy One visits us today, reaching out to us and enabling us to believe, even when we don't understand. Sometimes knowledge comes after we believe. At other times we take it all on faith, trusting the Just and Holy One to do those things that are right.

When the Holy touches us, those questions about understanding may not disappear, but they have less effect. When I see rampant injustice, or read about the murder of the innocent, or hear of an earthquake that kills thousands, I don't understand. Even so, I believe in a just and loving God. In recent years, when I find things of this nature perplexing me, I pray this way: "Enable me to accept the things beyond my understanding."

Do you think Thomas ever understood how the Resurrection occurred? Do you think he ever figured out how the Holy Spirit transformed Jesus? Probably not.

He didn't need to understand. He believed, and that was enough.

CHAPTER NINE

IN ANOTHER
FORM

As I have already mentioned, for nearly six years my wife and I lived in Kenya. Because of similarities in culture and customs, many biblical stories came alive to me during those years of missionary service. For me, one of the easiest stories to grasp occurs in the last chapter of Luke's gospel.

It's the road to Emmaus story, and one that never fails to remind me of our first four years in the southeastern section of Kenya, near Lake Victoria, known as Nyanza. We had one main road that led from the lake and hooked up with the other two-lane road, and that led to two major cities. I traveled by car, bus, motorcycle, or occasionally bicycle and sometimes even walked along the unpaved road. During the rainy season, the trucks scarred the clayish soil with deep pockmarks. In the dry season, wind blew dust so thick we had to bathe and change clothes after every trip.

Several times when I walked to the makeshift post office, three miles from where we lived, I'd have one or two companions along the way. I didn't invite them to walk with me; I didn't need to. If I was going east and they were going east and both at about the same time, we just naturally fell into step together. It would have been an act of rudeness not to greet them and then walk together. The fact that they were strangers was irrelevant. Because we traveled the same road, why not do it together? This happened to me on numerous occasions.

When I read the story of the two disciples going from Jerusalem to Emmaus, I can close my eyes and see a third man join them, the three then walking together along the road. They talk freely and pass on news they've heard.

That's how this story is set up. It's Sunday afternoon, the day of Jesus' resurrection. Two men, one of whom is called Cleopas and another who is unnamed, trudge the seven miles to Emmaus—probably about a two-hour walk. Somewhere en route a stranger joins them. The two men, obviously believers, are discussing the events in Jerusalem, and Jesus, whom they do not recognize, catches up and asks what they're talking about.

Luke says they stop. With sad voices and forlorn faces, Cleopas acts surprised at the question. He says that the stranger must be the only person in Jerusalem who doesn't know what's going on.

They don't know they're talking to Jesus. Luke says that when Jesus comes up to them, "their eyes were kept from recognizing him" (24:16). Mark doesn't tell the story but alludes to it this way: "After this he [Jesus] appeared in another form to two of them, as they were walking into the country. And they went back and told the rest, but they did not believe them" (Mark 16:12).

In some way that we can't explain or understand, Jesus walks with the two men and plies them with questions to get them discussing their disappointment. They share their now-dashed hopes with "Jesus of Nazareth, who was a prophet mighty in deed and word before God and all the people" (Luke 24:19). They tell him that the priests and other leaders conspired to condemn the prophet and had him crucified. "But we had hoped that he was the one to redeem Israel" (24:21). The two travelers go on to say that some women reported Jesus was no longer in the burial tomb and that an angel had declared Jesus was alive. The disciples rushed to the empty tomb, but they didn't find Jesus. They're troubled over the reports and don't believe what they've heard.

I want to pause here and focus on Cleopas. He's obviously a believer and one who has deep faith in Jesus as the Messiah. He knows the tomb is empty, but that's hardly enough to convince him of the Resurrection. The fact that angels were supposed to have told the women that Jesus was alive, he could easily discount as a hysterical reaction to their grief. No, as far as Cleopas is concerned, Jesus is dead.

It's all over. Hope is gone.

This is where the Holy creeps into the scene. Cleopas and his friend have, as they say in the addiction field, hit bottom. They're totally disillusioned. "It's all over, and we were wrong," I can hear them say. "This faith is nothing; we were deceived; Jesus failed us."

I can feel with them. They have wagered their lives on the promises of Jesus being the Messiah. How can a dead man fulfill the divine covenant? He can't, so that ends everything. Jesus lost his life. Once this happened, there was nothing left to believe.

✧

Once again, in the story of the walk to Emmaus, Cleopas doesn't grasp that Jesus is walking beside him the entire time. He moans and cries out in his disappointment, utterly unaware of the Messiah's presence. As I read the story centuries after the fact, I'm amazed that they don't catch on, but Luke tells us that God prevented them from recognizing Jesus.

The stranger listens to the litany of events and then says, "Oh, how foolish you are, and how slow of heart to believe all that the prophets have declared!" (24:25). From that introduction, Jesus teaches them the gospel message, beginning with the story of Moses.

They still don't recognize that the Messiah walks beside them.

It's almost dark when they arrive at Emmaus, and the two men urge Jesus to stop and eat with them. When they share food together, their eyes are opened. They get the message. The Holy has broken through with reality.

Luke tells this section briefly: "When he was at table with

them, he took bread, blessed and broke it, and gave it to them. Then their eyes were opened, and they recognized him; and he vanished from their sight" (24:30–31).

One version says that he disappeared. We don't know how he vanished, but we know that Jesus didn't leave until after they had their moment of insight—until they *knew*. In the act of receiving and eating food with Jesus comes the divine breakthrough. Just that quickly they grasp what Jesus had been teaching for more than three years.

That's when we discern the Holy invading. The enlightenment doesn't come through logical study or analytical scrutiny. It's an instantaneous experience. The two men listen to Jesus talk to them for a couple of hours. During that time they absorb information, but they still don't recognize him. They hang on to every word, but they still don't perceive who is teaching them.

After Jesus disappears, "They said to each other, 'Were not our hearts burning within us while he was talking to us on the road, while he was opening the scriptures to us?' " (24:32). This event also implies that once we grasp insight, we can look backward and say, "Oh, yes, that's what it meant." It's like the clue left on page 9 of a mystery novel that makes no sense until page 307. Then we say, "Oh, sure, I get it now."

❧

As I ponder the story of the Road to Emmaus, it makes me aware that one of the methods of the Pursuing One is to push us through dark places. We need moments of spiritual blindness before our eyes can be opened to divine truths. Is it possible that sometimes we need to agonize? To face disappointments? To live with uncertainty? And isn't it just as possible that the Holy sometimes comes to us in a different form—in ways we wouldn't have considered or contemplated?

How does the Relentless One chase after us today in another form? I'll give three examples.

First, when God uses the words of a stranger. During the early years of our marriage Shirley and I lived on the north side of Chicago, and I taught in the public schools. For a couple of years I regularly took our clothes to one particular dry cleaner. I don't recall the reason, but we started going to a different dry cleaner. Perhaps three years later I took clothes to the first place again. Three people were in line ahead of me.

We were going through a particularly difficult time in our lives. Both Shirley and I felt the call to go to East Africa as missionaries. A number of problems erupted, and it looked as if the door had slammed in our faces.

That day as I stood in line, I had hit a low point. No matter how hard I'd tried, nothing had worked. I didn't know which way to turn. I kept asking God to speak to me, to give me a sign, to give me some kind of encouragement. I had been seeking the way for several days.

Just then the woman who had been at the front of the line

turned to leave. She nodded to me, but I was too self-absorbed to pay much attention. "You remind me of someone," she said and stared at me through extremely thick glasses. "He used to come in here and was always smiling."

I recognized the woman from years before and realized she was referring to me, but I didn't know what to say so I just gazed at her.

"I never knew his name," she continued, "but I knew God was with him." She patted my shoulder and walked away.

That elderly woman delivered the divine message. In those few sentences the Divine Pursuer had lifted my spirits. *God was with me.* That's the different form God used. This may sound strange, but in that instant I knew the door would open for us to go to Africa. Within a year we landed in Nairobi.

Second, sometimes a Bible verse grabs us; this is what one friend calls the inner witness. I tend to want to discount such verses if they're pulled out of context or refer to something that seems to have no relevance. Yet here's a story that had a powerful impact.

I met a nurse-in-training named Lois at a Bible study group; she struggled with her faith. She commented once, "I wish the Holy Spirit would speak to me through the Bible— just once—and I'll never doubt him again."

A few weeks later a beaming Lois said, "God spoke to me through a Bible verse last night. And he called me by name!" She read the verse taken out of context, but the Relentless One owns those words and has sovereign control over the way they're used.

"It's the last part of the final verse of Matthew." She paused and went on. "My name is Lois, but my family always calls me Lo, so that's why this verse is so powerful. Jesus said, 'And, *lo,* I am with you alway, even unto the end of the world'" (Matthew 28:20 KJV).

She laughed and giggled and read the verse aloud again. "I know that's not what Jesus was saying then, but I believe it is what Jesus is saying to me now."

Lois didn't say so, but the Divine Pursuer had worked a miracle. For the several months until she finished her training and moved out of state, she radiated the peace she had found in Jesus Christ.

Third, we sit in church discouraged, hardly aware of what's going on, and then the words of a hymn or maybe a single sentence from the pulpit rips at our hearts.

When I called my mother long-distance to tell her that Shirley and I, together with our three young children, were going to Africa as missionaries, she said little, but I knew she didn't like what she heard. Fighting had broken out in Congo, and some speculated it might spread all over the continent.

After my call, Mom sat alone in the living room for a couple of hours. Darkness streaked across the sky, but she couldn't move. "How can I give him up?" she prayed. "How can this be your will to let them go over there? Who knows what will happen to Cec and his family?"

She cried for several minutes, pleading either for peace or for God to show me I was mistaken. Exhausted from prayer and wearied with crying, she closed her eyes and stared into the darkness. Just then she became aware that on her radio, tuned to the Moody network station, they were playing hymns. She heard one or two, but nothing spoke to her. She got out of her rocking chair to turn off the radio, and then she heard these words:

Jesus shall reign where'er the sun
Does his successive journeys run,
His kingdom spread from shore to shore,
'Til moons shall wax and wane no more.[1]

Tears streamed down her cheeks. That was Mom's moment to surrender me and to stop resisting God. The Holy Spirit had pursued her, but it took that message—a word in a different form—for her to hear. Jesus Christ was reigning in Africa and everywhere else in the world. She didn't need to fear for us: We were in perfect hands.

Yes, God appears in different forms at different times in our lives. Perhaps that's one reason the Christian faith remains exciting—the Relentless One never runs out of ways to grab our attention, to teach us, and, when necessary, to chase us. The Jesus-in-Another-Form who appeared to the two disciples on the road to Emmaus is the same one who comes to us in a variety of ways.

More than the variety of ways and the different forms, it

is important to realize that divine love refuses to let us go. If we can't or won't hear the message one way, our always-loving, always-pursuing God sends the word to us in another form.

CHAPTER TEN

MORE THAN THESE?

I'm an expressive person—at least that's my way of saying it. When I was a kid I had to find words to say everything. It wasn't until I was in seminary that Wade Huie, one of my professors, confronted me: "You think you can cover everything with words, don't you?"

His words shocked me, especially because he taught homiletics. "How else . . . how else do you explain or understand things?" I asked.

"Not always with words," he said, and the conversation ended.

The fact that I remember the incident clearly says it was a significant one. It's taken me years to realize that verbal expressions aren't always enough. They are, after all, only symbols, but many of us grasp them as the ultimate in understanding others and their actions. No matter how difficult the problem or situation, I used to believe that if I could find exactly the right expression, the perfect sentence, I could correct the matter.

My "non-expressive" friends have smiled indulgently because they function well without a lot of verbiage, and they sometimes have tried to tell me, "Your words get in the way. You get so busy talking, I can't figure out what's going on."

They value silence, a tender expression, a sigh, a wink, or a raised eyebrow. They rely on their intuitive perceptions. As one expert said, "They hear with a third ear, and they hear what isn't being said."

If you're an expressive type like me, you can readily understand Peter's dilemma after the Resurrection. If you're less verbal, I hope you'll feel more kindly toward us that are still learning. Peter was an expressive man—he always seemed to have something to say when silence developed or Jesus asked a question.

As I pointed out in an earlier chapter, early in his relationship with Jesus, Peter cries out, "Get away from me! I'm a sinful man!" Another person in the same situation might have quaked, hunched his shoulders, and turned his shame-laden face away from the Master. Another might have wept. We all use the tools that come naturally to us. For Peter, I believe his words were tools.

On another occasion, Jesus asks his disciples who people say he is. They respond with a variety of answers from Elijah to John the Baptist. Then Jesus presses, "But who do you say that I am?" (Matthew 16:15).

Words flow from the expressive Peter's mouth: "You are

the Messiah, the Son of the living God" (16:16). That comment receives commendation from Jesus, who says, in effect, "You haven't reasoned out that answer; it has come to you straight from my Father in heaven" (16:17).

On another occasion, Jesus miraculously feeds five thousand men, plus women and children. Afterward he speaks to his many followers and some leave, saying, "[His] teaching is difficult; who can accept it?" (John 6:60). Jesus continues to reveal more about future events; then he pauses and stares at the twelve before he asks, "Do you also wish to go away?" (6:67).

Again Peter rushes in with the right response. Before the others have even thought it through, he blurts out, "Lord, to whom can we go? You have the words of eternal life. We have come to believe and know that you are the Holy One of God" (6:69).

These are powerful words of faith, expressive of his commitment, and they not only evidence boldness but also hint of his later leadership. There are other instances of Peter with his famous foot-in-mouth habit of speaking too quickly. All of these experiences define the character of Peter, and we have no difficulty understanding why he became the head of the twelve. He was quick, articulate, and perceptive—all outstanding leadership qualities. Whenever we read that Jesus wants to be away from the crowds, he takes his little group, his inner circle: Peter, James, and John. The gospel writers always list Peter's name first.

Peter, the stalwart leader, the great apostle, finally faces his greatest test. For months Jesus has been speaking of his own death and resurrection. As the gospel writers point out, even though Peter had moments of insight that Jesus was the Messiah, none of the disciples comprehended the meaning of what the Lord said to them. Maybe they didn't understand what they weren't ready to accept.

On the night of Jesus' betrayal by Judas, all the disciples run away when the authorities come to arrest Jesus. Hours earlier, in the Upper Room, Peter had vowed that while the others might fail, he would remain true: "Even though I must die with you, I will not deny you" (Matthew 26:35). The other disciples promise the same thing, but it's Peter on whom the spotlight focuses.

After Jesus' arrest, within minutes Peter denies three times that he knows the Lord. Matthew's account ends, "And [Peter] went out and wept bitterly" (26:75).

The writers go into detail on the story of Jesus' crucifixion and resurrection. Afterward Jesus makes several appearances. It's interesting to note that Peter and Jesus never seem to be alone during any of these encounters. The first three Gospels pass over any specific mention of Peter, but John gives us two accounts where Peter is present.

In the first place, Jesus appears in the Upper Room and shows his wounded hands to Thomas. The second occurrence takes place at the Sea of Tiberias (also known as the Sea of Galilee or Lake Gennesaret), where seven of the disciples go fishing. (See John 21.) It's another empty-nets story; they do what Jesus tells them, casting on the right side of the boat, and when they obey, they come up with a large catch. When Peter realizes that it's Jesus on the shoreline, he dives overboard and swims to land. Jesus has a fire going, and they share broiled fish for breakfast.

Afterward comes the memorable story of Peter being touched by the Divine Pursuer, and in a more profound way than he had been before. The account is remarkably straightforward and simple.

Before I focus on the event itself, think about Peter and Jesus. Can you imagine how Peter must have been feeling after the Resurrection? Everyone considered him the leader of the twelve, and this meant he was supposed to set the example. He's the one who boasted that he would die alongside Jesus rather than deny him. He's the man who realized his weakness and wept bitterly. Assuming he and Jesus have not spoken to each other alone since the betrayal, how can this man grasp that he is already forgiven? He will eventually come to realize that when Jesus surrendered his life on the cross, God declared Peter righteous.

Whether he comprehends this or not, there is also the issue of forgiving himself. Although Jesus has forgiven him, can Peter let go of his sin?

I ask that question because this is where most of us struggle. We fail, we say harsh words, we do deeds that dishonor God, and then we confess. If anyone asks, we quickly affirm our orthodoxy and say, "Of course, God has forgiven me. I've confessed my sin and it's gone." What we often don't admit is that we're still holding out by not forgiving ourselves. We keep the memory of failure alive and refuse to enjoy God's grace.

Do you suppose Peter felt that way? He isn't the only disciple to vow faithfulness. He isn't the only one to run away after the Romans capture Jesus. He is, however, the leader of the others. He expected better of himself. Perhaps he can't accept that Jesus can forgive him for rashly vowing loyalty and then only hours later denying any knowledge of the Lord.

How does Jesus forgive him in such a way that Peter grasps the message? How can Jesus make this clear to an expressive person in a way that makes the deepest impression? I wonder if words are enough.

My explanation of the final scene in John's gospel is that Jesus transcends the expressive. He speaks, but he's saying far more than the words John records.

I want to look at the scene, and instead of quoting it, I'm going to paraphrase. My reason is the use of the word "love" in English (we have only one word). The Greek language has *four* words for love, and two of them appear in the New Testament. The first, in verbal form, is *philéo,* which I like to translate "fond of."

The second, in the verbal form *agapáo,* has nothing to do with emotions. It's an attitude, an intention. This is the word Jesus uses elsewhere when he commands us to love God with our total being and to love our neighbors as ourselves. Our Savior never commands us to *feel* a certain way; God does command us to *act* in prescribed ways. In telling this story, I'm translating *agapáo* as "committed to."

Jesus has cooked fish, and at least seven of the disciples are present and have eaten. As soon as breakfast is over, Jesus asks, "Peter, are you more *committed to* me than these?"

I have to pause here because the Greek doesn't make clear what "these" refers to. Some have assumed that Jesus is referring to the other disciples and asking, "Are you more committed to me than any of them?" That doesn't make sense to me. How could Peter possibly make that comparison?

How should he have answered in such a case? "Oh, Jesus, I'm more devoted to you than any of the others! Why, I've fully given you everything, but some of them have reservations." Not likely.

A more viable explanation is that Jesus referred to the elements of Peter's life—fishing, ministry, anything that takes the focus off Jesus himself. "Are you more *committed to* me, Peter, than you are to anything else in your life? Even more than your status as an apostle? Even more than your leadership role? Even more than ministering in my name? Even more than healing sick people? Even more than casting out demons?" This sounds like a sensible question.

"Jesus, you know I'm *fond of* you."

Here's where I see the Holy Pursuer on Peter's trail. Peter can't match Jesus' words; he can't make that kind of statement about his commitment. How could he? Would he dare? Surely he remembers too well the last time he boasted of his faith and his commitment: "No matter what any of the others do, you can count on me!" Now Peter faces himself, and he's aware of his failure.

"Feed my lambs, Peter." Jesus says those simple, commissioning words, but they don't sink in. So Jesus asks again, "Peter, are you *committed to* me?" After Peter again says, "I'm *fond of* you," Jesus adds, "Tend my sheep."

Jesus asks a third time, but this time the question is different—he drops down to Peter's word. "Peter, are you *fond of* me?"

Peter feels the sting of such a rebuke, and John adds an editorial note: "Peter felt hurt because he said [it] to him the third time" (21:17). Jesus commissions him once more to feed the sheep.

That's the story. If we can move beyond mere words to convey full meaning, we can easily see this as Jesus' way of touching an expressive person in a way that stretches him. If Jesus had said, "Peter, I forgive you," that might have taken care of everything.

Peter then might have re-declared his unworthiness. That's not what Jesus seeks here. Peter has been forgiven. This isn't a moment where the Savior cleanses his servant. This is a commissioning service. In the middle of this event, the expressive one moves beyond hearing the right words.

Something more important than speaking words transpires at the lakeside. It's about forgiveness, but in the sense that forgiveness is part of the foundation and not the total message. Jesus pushes Peter to internalize the message of the Resurrection. He wants his follower and friend to move beyond depending on words so that he can grasp what words cannot explain.

It's one of those incidents where an eyewitness tries to explain an event and finally says, "You'd have had to be there to understand." Isn't it possible that Peter receives a message from Jesus' presence that transcended his words? Did the apostle "hear" a message that went into the depth of his soul—a life-changing message that would start transforming him into a new person?

It must have taken a little time to sink in. We get no evidence of any change in Peter in the final verses of John's gospel. When we turn to the book of Acts, however, the Peter of the New Testament emerges. He is the bold and able leader, the one who feeds the sheep and leads the others. He's the one willing to take risks and who stands up to the Jewish leaders. No more running away or fearing to acknowledge Jesus.

This is where I see that the Holy Pursuer has captured and changed him; first of all, Peter faces forgiveness. That may sound trite, but I suspect he may have felt unworthy of being forgiven—as if his sin had been too serious for God to cleanse. *You should have known better*, his conscience would say. *You were with him for three years. He trusted you. You were his close companion. You are despicable, the worst disciple of all, Peter, because you denied the best friend you've ever had in your life.*

As the two men sit together, I believe Peter gets the

message. The Relentless One moves inside the man on a level he has not perceived before. So the exchange between the two really isn't about forgiveness. It's about acceptance, about service, and above all, about Peter's commitment. He's saying, "Peter, I trust you. I entrust the future leadership of the church into your hands and the hands of the others as you lead them onward."

In a subtle way, I think Jesus is saying that forgiveness is built into the commission. He has gone beyond taking away sin and is now calling him to service. Peter is still back at the realm of forgiveness and not ready for leadership and service.

"Are you committed?" Jesus asks. "Are you ready?"

"I like you, Jesus. I'm your friend." Peter says. He's still tugging away with issues of the past—issues Jesus has wiped away, while Peter still hangs on.

How incredibly modern this sounds. We carry around guilt and shame and allow them to get between God and us. Long ago the Savior passed over our failures and now focuses on our service and our commitment.

Here's a brief example from my own Christian life that may help clarify this. For perhaps the first twenty years of my Christian pilgrimage, I believed that I couldn't have a time of protracted prayer without first going through a rigorous self-examination of sin and failure. "If I regard iniquity in my heart, the Lord will not hear me" (Psalm 66:18 KJV) had been quoted and thrown at me in my early Christian days. I felt I had to clear up all sin before I had the right to talk to God.

It took me a long time to embrace the concept of grace, and this includes forgiveness. Of course I still confess sin, but I do it as I become aware of my failure or at times when I ask God to look at my heart. I no longer go through agonizing torment trying to find something to confess or of feeling I can't really pray without first going through torturous self-scrutiny. I accept the grace that says, "Your sins are forgiven. Go, and sin no more."

Isn't that the message of the Holy to Peter that day at the lake? "Peter, I'm not going to say I forgive you. That's taken care of. I'm calling you to service." Isn't this a message that extends beyond words?

It's a message that says, "You are forgiven. Now forgive yourself and serve me."

This is the result of one phase of the relentless pursuit. Peter had long been claimed; now he's ready for a deeper level of his relationship. As always, it seems the only way for Peter or his spiritual descendents today to tap into that new dimension is to experience further encounters with the God who refuses to let us go.

Here's how I envision this story ending. Before Jesus' ascension, Peter says to him, "Jesus, I am committed to you."

"Yes, I know that. Now feed my sheep. Do the work I've called you to do."

"You've forgiven me, haven't you?"

"Do you have to ask?" Jesus says and smiles.

CHAPTER ELEVEN

DYING GRACE

For years after my conversion I had tried to talk to Ray, my older brother, about Jesus Christ. Ray was a kind man and wouldn't have insulted me, but in his soft, quiet manner, he made it clear that he had no interest in discussing a relationship with God.

We lived in different states and didn't see each other often. The last time we spoke, he was lying in the hospital, dying of lung cancer. Again I tried to speak with him about spiritual issues, but he didn't want to listen. Most of the time he told me of his plans for the family after he recovered.

The day before Ray died, his wife asked a chaplain to talk with him. This time Ray listened, and he had a classic death-bed conversion. A few minutes after he passed away, his wife said to me, "He died with a smile on his face. I know he was ready. Why else would he be smiling?"

For years before Ray's death I had heard about what some

Christians referred to as dying grace—that special, loving touch of God that enables people to die well, and sometimes boldly.

One other experience of dying grace stands out in my mind. Shirley's mother suffered a massive stroke, and they assumed she wouldn't pull out of it. She survived, however, and her two daughters were preparing to take her home from the hospital. "It was wonderful," she said to them. "I felt so close to God, and I didn't want to come back. If this ever happens again, I want you to instruct the doctors not to revive me."

Mom Brackett spoke of her readiness to die. Actually it was more like eagerness. She had been a highly active woman, filled with life, but when the time came for her to prepare to leave this world, she wanted to go. I don't know what happened to her following that debilitating stroke, but it took away the fear of death and enabled her to look expectantly to something better.

Three days later she had a second stroke and died. All of us in the family were at peace. Mom had been ready, and despite our sense of loss we rejoiced in her joyous departure.

That's dying grace.

This illusive quality is something that comes to us only at the needed moment, yet it comes in such a way that all fear vanishes. We take joy in what lies ahead. In loving preparation to take his faithful ones home, God sometimes previews heaven and glory for them to look forward to—and as a witness to those who remain.

The best biblical example I can give is that of a man named Stephen, known as the first Christian martyr. No man in the Bible exemplifies dying grace more beautifully. The Holy Pursuing One touches him in such a way that in his dying moments he may have been a greater witness than he had been during his lifetime.

I want to look at the story of Stephen that brought him to his moment of dying grace. Stephen's name suddenly appears in Acts 6. During the early days of the church, Christians lived in a communal manner, sharing whatever they owned with each other. Daily they distributed food to widows and orphans.

The leaders finally face a crisis. What's the best way for Peter and the other apostles to spend their time? Should they serve food to the orphans and widows? Should they pray, study, and preach the Gospel? They make a pragmatic decision, and Peter declares, "It is not right that we should neglect the word of God in order to wait on tables" (Acts 6:2).

He then instructs believers to choose seven men to take over the food distribution business. It's also significant that they didn't ask for volunteers. He tells them to select "seven men of good standing, full of the Spirit and of wisdom" (6:3).

The first time I read that it amazed me. Peter wants them to be *Spirit-filled* just to serve food each day? They need *wisdom* to be a lowly person that carries dishes from the cooking pots to the tables? Isn't that like asking people who have doctoral degrees to hand out aspirin?

And yet that's part of the power of this whole account.

Stephen is the first name on the list: "What [the apostles] said pleased the whole community and they chose Stephen, a man full of faith and the Holy Spirit" (6:5), and then they list the other six men. Once chosen, they take the seven through a kind of commissioning service, which shows how seriously the first believers considered any responsibility: "They had these men stand before the apostles, who prayed and laid their hands on them" (6:6).

The impression readers get from Acts is that even then Stephen isn't just a man who has walked into the fellowship but one who has already proven himself. This strongly indicates that his daily duties are not beneath him or anything upon which he looks down. Anything done for God is service, whether private or public, small or large. Most of us know this, but we still get caught up in the megastar concept that the more high profile the ministry the greater the service and the more we please God. Stephen apparently doesn't think so; neither do the apostles.

A few verses later, we read, "Stephen, full of grace and power, did great wonders and signs among the people" (6:8). As the story unfolds—and it's the longest single narrative in the book of Acts—many of the Jewish leaders begin to plot against Stephen to stop him from preaching about Jesus. They go so far as to charge him and bring him before the Council (the Sanhedrin), where false witnesses testify against him.

Here's the significant test for a man like Stephen. His enemies confront and threaten him but he won't recant. He surely knows he'll die if he stands fast. Because his enemies work so diligently to charge him, it's obvious they want the judgment of the death sentence placed on him.

Luke makes a simple statement about Stephen in the midst of all the accusations: "And all who sat in the council looked intently at [Stephen], and they saw that his face was like the face of an angel" (6:15). He doesn't die on the spot, but this is the moment when even his enemies observe something in Stephen's face. This is Luke's way of talking about the powerful effect of Stephen's demeanor on those who stared at him.

Despite what they perceive, nothing changes them. If anything, they press their accusations more intensely. The entire seventh chapter of Acts contains Stephen's response to the charges. It's an unfinished sermon that takes up more than fifty verses. In essence, Stephen tells the Jewish leaders that the first time God speaks or tries to do something, the Jews reject the message, but they accept it the second time. When he blatantly called them murderers of Jesus, they "became enraged and ground their teeth at Stephen" (7:54). In the verses after that, we read that they grab Stephen, drag him outside the city, and stone him to death.

The important element is how Stephen reacts. Before his sermon, they stared at his beatific face. After he's interrupted in the middle of his defense, and just before they drag him out of the city, he says, "I see the heavens opened and the Son of Man standing at the right hand of God!" (7:56). The accusers cover their ears—such words are blasphemy to them—and mob violence takes over.

Stephen's prayer startles readers. Instead of cursing his accusers or moaning because he's dying so young, or that he's innocent and is being unjustly killed, Stephen kneels and prays, "Lord, do not hold this sin against them," and Luke adds, "When he had said this, he died" (7:60).

That's dying grace in the man Stephen. He has lived the faithful life and this becomes the final test of it—the way he loses his temporal life.

In those final moments, his single prayer is for those who have put him to death. Surely this has to be one of the most powerful touches of the Holy. Many of us can speak about the love and goodness of God. We can give all the orthodox responses to forgiveness. Yet here is one person, surrounded by dozens of hate-filled leaders. They scream at him, clench their fists, stone him, and have only one desire, and that's to snuff out his life.

He blesses them: That's dying grace! In fact, I assume that even in the midst of his body being pounded by those stones—and they don't throw small, hand-sized rocks either— he sees their faces, hears their angry threats, and feels their unmitigated wrath.

Unlike many of us, Stephen forgives. He prays for his enemies. Many of us tend to strike back with the same emotional response we receive. When someone lashes out at us in anger, our natural tendency is to meet their negative response with ours—and we raise the volume and intensity.

In that unforgettable moment when Stephen is giving up his life, the Relentless One—the One-Who-Never-Lets-Go—

holds the man close and touches him with dying grace. To ask God to forgive our killers isn't an ordinary human virtue. I can only imagine how powerfully his words impacted them.

I assume some of the Jewish leaders respond by picking up even larger boulders. They want to hasten his death and shut up the words of forgiveness. They hate the man and everything he stands for and preaches about. Others probably rush at him just as rapidly out of shame, refusing to allow any more condemnation to fill their minds and hearts.

Then Luke records that Stephen cries out with a loud voice, which makes us know that they hear his final words; they witness dying grace in Stephen.

When the Holy Pursuer touches a person in such a moment, it becomes a miracle. After an invasion of the Holy, all human venom is gone, and natural retaliation doesn't matter. Because the Relentless One endows him with dying grace, Stephen's last thoughts are for those who despise him and his God. His words echo those of the Savior he serves. Jesus himself had cried out, "Father, forgive them; for they do not know what they are doing" (Luke 23:34).

This dying grace does two significant things. First, we realize that it enables Stephen to leave this life with love and compassion. He says nothing to condemn them—even though they had bribed false witnesses to speak against him in court. That act alone was a violation of the ninth commandment not to bear false witness. They knew they had violated the sacred law of Moses; such a desperate measure results in cowardly and deplorable sins. Despite everything they can say or do against him, Stephen remains true to the One-Who-Won't-Let-Go.

Second, notice the effect of dying grace: The words soar and reach out beyond Stephen's death. Luke tells us that other believers took Stephen's body and buried it. To do such a loving act had to have been infused with great courage. If the officials killed Stephen, surely the lives of other followers of Jesus Christ were endangered as well. Luke leaves the impression that their own safety didn't matter. At that moment they wanted to honor their brother and give him a proper burial. Acts 8:2 also says that those disciples make "a loud lamentation," which means they didn't sneak away and have a secret burial for their fallen hero.

Something even more important deserves notice. Luke adds a few details at the end of this incident by turning attention to a bystander named Saul—who would later be known to the world as Paul, the great apostle of the early church. Here is the end of the story.

Stephen cries, "You stubborn and hardheaded people! You are always fighting against the Holy Spirit, just as your ancestors did. . . . Angels gave you God's Law, but you still don't obey it" (Acts 7:51, 53 CEV).

> The council members shouted and covered their ears. At once they all attacked Stephen and dragged him out of the city. Then they started throwing stones at him. *The men who had brought charges against him put their coats at the feet of a young man named Saul.* As Stephen was being stoned to death, he called out, "Lord Jesus, please welcome me!" He knelt down and shouted, "Lord, don't

blame them for what they have done." Then he died. *Saul approved the stoning of Stephen.* Some faithful followers of the Lord buried Stephen and mourned very much for him. (Acts 7:57–8:2 CEV, emphasis mine)

After the death and burial of Stephen, the disciples scatter over all the region, and belief in Jesus as the Messiah is no longer just a sect in and around Jerusalem. Philip, another of the seven men chosen to wait on tables, goes to Samaria, the northern neighbors who were of mixed race and detested by Jews. They listen, believe, and miracles take place.

But these events with Philip are a parenthesis that follows a statement about Saul after Stephen's burial: "Saul was ravaging the church by entering house after house; dragging off both men and women, he committed them to prison" (8:3).

Acts 9 begins:

> Meanwhile [while Philip was ministering in Samaria], Saul, still breathing threats and murder against the disciples of the Lord, went to the high priest and asked him for letters to the synagogues at Damascus, so that if he found any who belonged to the Way, men or women, he might bring them bound to Jerusalem. (9:1–2)

On the way to Damascus, a blinding light strikes Paul; he falls to the ground and hears the voice of Jesus. This becomes Paul's conversion. Yet Paul's story couldn't have taken place without Stephen's dying grace. Saul was not only the man who agreed with the execution; the language suggests he is an official who affirms the stoning. From the other statements we read about him, Saul is one of the most zealous Pharisees as well as someone who seeks to rid their religion of what he believes are corruptions and distortions of their historic faith.

We can only imagine the powerful impact that Stephen's death had on Saul. Certainly something about Stephen's words unforgettably impacts the zealot.

The Holy Pursuer touched Stephen on the last day of his life to prepare him to die, but part of that dying grace reaches out and clutches Saul, even though weeks probably pass before his conversion experience on the Damascus Road.

Augustine said, "The church owes Paul to the prayers of Stephen."

Yet who would believe that dying grace could produce such a powerful effect on a human life? Like Stephen, sometimes the greatest witnesses of God's saints are their deaths rather than their lives. Sometimes the proof of having been found by the God-Who-Pursues is for others to witness the radiance of a believer's death.

CHAPTER TWELVE

PURCHASING POWER

I knew him only as Wayne, but everyone talked about how much money he had and how heavily he gave to his church. Physically, he wasn't much to look at—a man in his fifties with graying hair, he wore hand-tailored suits over a flabby body.

I had gone to that church to teach a midweek Bible study for a few months. Wayne introduced himself, but I felt an aversion to him. Maybe it was because I saw so many people fawning over him. They greeted him with ingratiating words and did everything but bow in his presence. It appeared that most of the church members tried to say or do things to please him.

Then came an incident where I saw how people really felt—something about allowing an outside group to use the fellowship hall. He opposed it, and being chairman of the board of deacons, his decision usually became the decision of everyone else. More than once he had subtly implied (so I'm told) that if they wanted his support they'd have to "make the right choices."

On this occasion, however, one man openly disagreed with Wayne. So far as I know, it was the first time anyone had opposed him publicly. I wasn't on their church board, but at the next Bible study class I heard what had happened. The man who wanted the outside group to use the facilities explained that it was a Christian organization and that they were willing to pay if necessary.

Wayne adamantly refused. "This is our building. We paid for it; it's for our use. Let them find their own place."

The words between the men grew heated. Apparently Wayne said, "I give a lot of money to this church and I expect people to respect my wishes."

"You think you can pay for everything. You think you can buy your way into anything, even heaven, don't you?"

The end of the "discussion" came when Wayne said, "If you allow them or any other group to use our facilities, I will not put another dollar into this church."

"May your money perish with you!" yelled the other man.

Wayne stood up and said, "Unless this board votes unanimously with me—right now—I'm going to walk out the door, and I will not return to this church."

A hasty vote revealed only two men who would not be bullied. Even so, Wayne walked out, and so far as I know, he didn't return.

Just before our Bible study started, a number of church

members stood in a group and discussed the fiery event. Most of us heard the story from more than one source. Before we started the study we prayed, and two people asked the Holy Spirit to soften Wayne's heart. I suspect that a lot of them were praying that he would not stay away—his giving more than equalized the total of the other two hundred and fifty members.

As supposedly objective outsiders, we can shake our heads at this story. What kind of Christian was Wayne? Did he think he could buy God's favor? Did he believe that money alone was sufficient?

I thought of Wayne again when I was reading about a man usually referred to as Simon Magus, whose story occurs in Acts 8. I noticed many similarities in their approach to the Christian life.

⟨⟩

After the death of Stephen, persecution spread and the disciples left their original area. It had always been God's plan for believers to go throughout the entire world, but in the earliest days of the church they had remained in Jerusalem. Jesus said just before his ascension, "You will receive power when the Holy Spirit has come upon you; and you will be my witnesses in Jerusalem, in all Judea and Samaria, and to the ends of the earth" (Acts 1:8). The disciples stayed at home until persecution forced them out.

Philip, one of the seven chosen along with Stephen to be

a deacon, went to Samaria and preached. Going to that nation, just north of Judea, was worse than entering foreign soil. The Jews and Samaritans (who were of mixed Jewish and Gentile blood) had been enemies for centuries. Their quarrel began in the eighth century B.C. when the Assyrians conquered the northern kingdom of Israel (with its capital at Samaria). As conquerors did in those days, the Assyrians transported the greater part of the population into foreign areas and brought in strangers to settle the land. These strangers intermarried with the remaining Jews.

Two centuries later, the Babylonians overpowered the southern kingdom (of Judah) and carried the rest of the Jews to Babylon. Those who went, however, refused to lose their identity; they retained their religious and ethnic heritage. When the exiles returned to rebuild their devastated city under Ezra and Nehemiah, those in Samaria offered to help. Because of their racial mixture—which they apparently considered an unforgivable crime—the faithful Jews refused. From that time on the two groups remained bitter rivals.

Despite the centuries of animosity between the two cultures, Philip preaches in Samaria, the place where most Jews wouldn't even pause to eat. As he tells them about Jesus Christ, miracles and healings take place, and many believe. After Philip sends word of the happenings back to Jerusalem, the leaders authorize Peter and John to go there.

Among the new believers in Samaria is a magician named Simon. He's not really that unusual; people regularly consulted astrologers, prophets, medicine men, and magicians for guidance and healing. Whether such results were because of their having tapped into evil powers, pure trickery, or a kind of psychology isn't the point. People listened, believed, and paid them for their services.

Apparently Simon stood out as being especially gifted at his craft. This is the kind of situation into which Philip intrudes. As a stranger and a Jew, he must have demonstrated boldness and courage to proclaim the Gospel. As the writer of Acts points out, great signs and wonders accompany his message. After those miracles occur, people turn to God.

Luke puts it this way:

> The crowds with one accord listened eagerly to what was said by Philip, hearing and seeing the signs that he did, for unclean spirits, crying with loud shrieks, came out of many who were possessed, and many others who were paralyzed or lame were cured. So there was great joy in that city. (Acts 8:6–8)

This is a time of God's demonstrated power, and the Holy Spirit does one outstanding miracle after another. The people see bodies made well; individuals possessed by demon spirits are restored to their right minds. All the accounts throughout the book of Acts show the Spirit working mightily. When people see this power at work, they believe and are changed.

Simon, among the most highly respected magicians, becomes a convert as well. He sees these things happen, which is what brings him to accept and believe in a power greater than his magic. Luke's presentation of him doesn't imply that he used trickery, although he may have:

> Now a certain man named Simon had previously practiced magic in the city and amazed the people of Samaria, saying that he was someone great. All of them, from the least to the greatest, listened to him eagerly, saying, "This man is the power of God that is called Great." And they listened eagerly to him because for a long time he had amazed them with his magic. (8:9–11)

It's important to emphasize that this was a high-profile man of Samaria; people flocked to him for help. If we don't grasp that miracles were occurring, we miss much of what's going on. When Philip comes, Simon hears the message, but in this case, he sees something—a power that exceeds his own. "Even Simon himself believed. After being baptized, he stayed constantly with Philip and was amazed when he saw the signs and great miracles that took place" (8:13).

When I read such an account, I have no trouble visualizing the practices of wizards and magicians. I met some men who practiced divination or magic during our years in Africa when many still went to witch doctors. Usually the witch doctors gave them strange potions made from the powder of rhino horns, an egg from an exotic bird, or a charm to protect them from malaria. Sometimes those things worked; it may have been because they simply believed what they heard and it came true—self-fulfilling prophecy. Many who lived in the more primitive areas and had little or no education and no modern facilities relied on witch doctors for healing or guidance.

On two different occasions witch doctors came to our meetings and surrendered to Jesus Christ. In both instances they asked church leaders to go to their homes with them and destroy the tools of their former trade.

I also have no question about the sincerity of Simon. He's a man who knows more about the beyond-natural happenings, miracles, healings, signs, and wonders than the general public. If Philip had been a fraud, Simon would have exposed him. I'm even willing to say that the magician did great deeds, or at least possessed unusual abilities.

When Philip arrives, what Simon witnesses must have made the man's eyes bulge, and he would have shaken his head in utter amazement. "This is truly God at work," he might have said. He believes, and Philip probably accepted the man's statement of faith. Although in the first days of the church the believers received baptism quite readily and without a lot of teaching, Philip was a man of great faith and a man who was guided and empowered by the Holy Spirit. He would have the discernment to spot a fraud.

Another element that's important to this story is that Simon receives baptism—which means not only that Philip believes him but also that Simon makes a strong public statement to the world—to the people he had formerly amazed. This declaration of faith dries up his source of income and he publicly denounces his former ways.

❧

Again I'll relate this to the more primitive areas of Africa where I lived. After the evangelists and pastors within a geographic area had a number of believers, perhaps as many as one hundred, they arranged a communal baptism. I participated in a few of them, and I saw how significant such an event could be for the crowd, including non-believers.

African leaders lined up the new converts, and as we sang hymns they formed a single line and walked to the edge of the river. We sang for about half an hour so that people all over the area could hear the music and come and observe. Not only did church members congregate but non-believers often outnumbered them. This was a big event, something that didn't take place often. While the Christians sang, the curious stayed, watched, and often sang with them.

After one of the leaders preached a brief message to explain the importance of baptism, one by one, the new converts walked into the water where two or three evangelists immersed them. Immediately after the last person was baptized, one of the evangelists faced the crowd and preached about Jesus Christ. I never saw one of those baptismal services end without many people coming forward and asking for prayer and salvation.

❧

It likely wasn't all that different in Philip's day. He preaches and demonstrates the power of God. Quite likely, he prays for a number of sick people who receive immediate healing, and delivers some from demonic powers. Whatever Philip did and whatever the results, Simon—a professional magician—believes. He observes and senses a spiritual power beyond anything he has known.

Later Peter and John arrive to verify the results and to see the workings of the Spirit. As I pointed out above, because of the racial hatred, there would have had to be a lot of evidence for Peter and John to accept that Samaritans would listen to a Jew talk about Jesus Christ, especially a Jew who is also the Messiah.

Luke states that the Holy Spirit had not yet come upon the new believers in Samaria. He's obviously referring to the story in Acts 2 where the Spirit of God descended on the day of Pentecost and the believers began to speak in other languages. In the early church the coming of the Spirit was connected with definite and visible phenomena; in particular, the people spoke in tongues. (This occurs in Acts 10:44–46 and again in chapter 20.) When the Holy Spirit did come upon people, they experienced an ecstasy that manifested itself, because they spoke words that, at least to the speaker, were meaningless. To the hearers, however, they were obvious languages.

Something supernatural had to have happened. Regardless of how people feel about such phenomena today, we can be quite sure such things occurred there. First, the Bible has other passages that support this. Second, as I've pointed out, something stronger than Simon's magic had to have been at work.

There's a third reason: This is also for the benefit of Peter and John, and consequently for the infant church, to see that the Spirit wanted them to go worldwide with the gospel. Christian Jews knew they were the divinely chosen nation and had grown up believing that Yahweh loved only one race of people. This experience is like a preview: It's not until later (see Acts 10) that Peter finally grasps the truth that the gospel message is for Jews *and* non-Jews. That happens when he is invited to the home of Cornelius, a Roman.

> While Peter was still speaking, the Holy Spirit fell upon all who heard the word. The circumcised believers [the Jews] who had come with Peter were astounded that the gift of the Spirit had been poured out even on the Gentiles, for they heard them speaking in tongues and extolling God. Then Peter said, "Can anyone withhold the water for baptizing these people who have received the Holy Spirit just as we have?" (Acts 10:44–47)

The new believers receive baptism, and later Peter defends his actions before the Jerusalem leaders with the proof of their speaking in foreign tongues. I stress this because something had to have happened to convince all the people involved that the Holy Spirit had come.

This takes us to the real point of the relentless pursuit of Simon Magus.

Peter and John lay their hands on the Samaritan believers,

and when they do, the people receive the Holy Spirit. "Now when Simon saw that the Spirit was given through the laying on of the apostles' hands, he offered them money" (Acts 8:18).

This is where many people condemn Simon, the former magician, and often don't finish reading the story. He did try to give Peter money for this phenomenal gift, saying, "Give me also this power so that anyone on whom I lay my hands may receive the Holy Spirit" (8:19).

In straightforward terms, Peter rebukes him:

> You and your money will both end up in hell if you think you can buy God's gift! You don't have any part in this, and God sees that your heart isn't right. Get rid of these evil thoughts and ask God to forgive you. I can see that you are jealous and bound by your evil ways. (Acts 8:20–23 CEV)

Here is Simon's response, a fact often overlooked: "Please pray to the Lord, so that what you said won't happen to me" (8:24 CEV).

The biblical account doesn't give the end of the story. Simon isn't the focus of the narrative, and Luke tells us that Peter and John went back to Jerusalem and preached in the Samaritan villages on the way. The obvious implication—and the only one that makes sense—is that they pray for Simon. The Holy One has brought deep conviction to him through the words of Peter, which probably scare him.

Think about Peter's rebuke. Simon was a baptized believer, and he's been following Philip around before the two apostles arrive. Nothing in the account suggests fraud or deception on the man's part. And yet when he sees the power of the apostles, he wants it. Why not? He was a man used to wielding power and being influential within the community.

He was honest about what he desired. We also need to remind ourselves that Simon is a new convert. When he sees this marvelous gift of the apostles, why wouldn't he want it? And if he wants it, isn't buying it the most natural way to obtain what he desires? Quite likely, that was the commercial system he had known in the past.

This is when the Holy One strikes hard: "You can't buy my power" is the message Simon hears, even if not the literal words. *He repents*. Simon shows his change of heart by begging them to pray that God will not punish him and that he'll not perish in hell.

The Relentless Pursuer encounters Simon and changes him in that moment. He sees the folly of his ways; that is, he sees how power can blind him and move him away from his commitment. He realizes he can't buy any of the gifts of God.

In this instance of a holy encounter, maybe he figures out the problem. He wants spiritual gifts and he wants to be used by God—a noble passion. His problem is that he has tried to get spiritual gifts the wrong way. Even if we assume he wants to use them for the good of others, he's still trying to get them in an incorrect fashion.

Let's jump to the present and think about the message that Simon heard.

At the beginning of this chapter, I told the story of a rich man named Wayne. I have no reason to think he wasn't a born-again Christian. I do think he had his priorities mixed up and his eyes in the wrong place. He tried to buy his way into the grace of God. Buying and bribing simply don't work in the spiritual realm, and we know this. We can smugly point fingers at such people. Their ways and methods are so clear. Or are they?

In the late 1990s I began to question how obvious this is. At the time I faced a situation where I knew what I wanted. Naturally I began to pray for God to guide. I went a little further: I told the Lord how much I wanted this thing to happen.

Nothing changed. A few days later I cried out more fervently and started listing the reasons I deserved this. I went down a long list of my past accomplishments for God, such as my faithfulness in church attendance, the activities I volunteered for, my giving, my Bible reading, examples of doing things for Jesus because they were the right things to do, even when I didn't want to do them. When I paused to think of more ammunition to load my spiritual guns and fire away at God's reluctance, I started to laugh.

I had been trying to bribe God! How could I do such a thing? How could I dare use my past faithfulness and accomplishments as a means to "pay" for divine favors?

Had I ever done this before? Then a stronger insight came.

Yes, I had tried—hundreds of times. Now, at least, I became aware of what I was doing. I wasn't ready to rely on grace or leave it up to God to choose. I wanted things done my way and within my time frame. To ensure that the Holy Spirit would honor my worthy request, I fortified it by hauling out my spiritual faithfulness as if to say, "Repay me for my virtuous life." I didn't use these words, but in effect I was saying, "You owe me. I've paid for this by my good deeds."

Was I really any different than Simon the magician? Or from Wayne the rich man? Probably not. Some think money will bring them God's favor. If they give large enough amounts to the Lord's work, surely the showers of heavenly blessings will flow. Some of us aren't that gullible; we offer our record of faithfulness and our commitments.

The Holy grabbed Simon when Peter rebuked him. He realized the error of his ways—and his words sound as if he's terrorized by the possibility of endless torment. We may not all hear the voice that says, "You'll perish in torment if you think you can buy God's favor." We're so much more subtle. We don't really want to "buy" God's favor. We just want to bribe the divine Blesser. If we can do enough and rack up enough "glory points," then surely God will honor our requests.

Here again are Peter's words to Simon:

> You and your money will both end up in hell if you think you can buy God's gift! You don't have any part in this, and God sees that your heart isn't right. Get rid of

these evil thoughts and ask God to forgive you. I can see that you are jealous and bound by your evil ways. (Acts 8:20–21 CEV)

If we substitute the word *work* or *deeds,* the Holy Pursuer may be shouting the same message at us. However, like Simon, we can declare our sin and God will forgive us.

The Holy also reminds us that while the Holy Spirit gives lovingly and freely, the same God also withholds out of wisdom. Maybe, like Simon of old, we'll sense the pursuit by the Holy and realize that bribery not only doesn't work, it's also the wrong approach. Maybe we need to learn to say, "Heavenly Father, this is what I'd like to have. May it please you to give it to me."

As we realize that the loving embrace of the God-Who-Pursues holds us tightly, we don't have to beg for grace or gifts. We will be able to ask as children who are loved by their heavenly Parent, and we no longer have to struggle to convince the Lord that we're worth listening to.

I think Simon understood.

I hope we do as well.

CHAPTER THIRTEEN

HEARKENING TO THE HOLY

How do you share something so special that you can't put the experience into expression? It's so sacred that you're afraid people will misunderstand it or try to copy it. How do you talk about a moment with God that is so powerful it totally changes your life, and yet you don't want to boast? What a terrible dilemma that must be—wanting to explain and yet not being able to make it clear.

Paul makes an attempt at explaining the unexplainable when he writes an extremely personal message in 2 Corinthians 12, where he speaks of being transported into the third heaven. After we read the account, we still have no clear idea of his actual experience, although the passage leaves the impression that some all-consuming encounter with the Holy took place. Paul was never the same again.

We don't even know when this happened to him. One

possibility is that he refers to his experience on the road to Damascus. Although I believe Paul did have a profound encounter there—and I mention this below—the experience he writes about came years afterward; he writes of an abundance of revelations that implies they came over a period of time.

Let's start with the initial breaking through of the Relentless Pursuer into his life. Paul (then called Saul of Tarsus) left Jerusalem with letters from the high priest, traveling toward Damascus. His purpose was to capture members of the new sect of Judaism that believed in Jesus Christ.

To prepare for this story in Acts 9, we have to reexamine (in chapters 7 and 8) the story of Stephen, the first martyr for the faith. As almost a by-the-way statement, Luke adds, "Saul approved of their killing [Stephen]" (Acts 8:1). We learn that after Stephen's death the Christians, now afraid, flee everywhere, and Saul "was ravaging the church by entering house after house; dragging off both men and women, he committed them to prison" (8:3).

Instead of following Saul/Paul, the book of Acts shifts the focus to Philip's travels to Samaria and the Gospel being proclaimed, and the chapter concludes with the conversion story of an Ethiopian cabinet minister. This follows the pattern laid down by Jesus for the believers to go from Jerusalem and Judea to Samaria and then to the rest of the world (cf. Acts 1:8). Chapter 9 begins this way: "Meanwhile, Saul, still breathing threats and murder against the disciples of the Lord . . ." Again, he had received documents that gave him permission to persecute those who were followers of "the Way" (as believers apparently were called in the early days).

On the road, the Relentless One grabs Paul, which Luke records this way: "Suddenly a light from heaven flashed around him. He fell to the ground and heard a voice" (9:3–4). The voice (who, after Saul inquires, identifies himself as Jesus—9:5) asks, "Why do you persecute me?" (9:4).

Apparently the others don't hear the words, but when Saul gets up from the ground, he's blind. The voice tells him that he's to go to Damascus, where he'll be further directed. This sounds almost like an espionage tale.

For three days the sightless Saul doesn't eat or drink; finally the Holy Spirit speaks to a disciple named Ananias, telling him to go to the blinded man. Reluctantly and fearfully, Ananias obeys, lays his hands on Saul, and the man's sight is restored.

This becomes a tale of miraculous conversion. Saul changes, and after a few days of instruction, he starts telling people about Jesus. The Jews try to kill Paul, but he escapes by hiding in a large basket while believers lower him over the city wall.

This is definitely an awesome encounter; in a sovereign manner, the Relentless Pursuer breaks through. Paul doesn't attend a gospel meeting or read a tract on salvation—the Holy bypasses everything and zaps the man while he's preparing to persecute believers in Damascus.

What went on during those three days of blindness and fasting, we have no idea. My assumption is that God had to humble Paul, one of the best-educated men of his day. This intellectually astute man had to receive instructions from the simple Ananias. The Divine Chaser broke through there as well, because he appeared to Ananias in a vision—breaking down his resistance and taking an unusual method to get to Saul/Paul.

As important as the event is, I don't think this is the source of Paul's great experience (being transported into the third heaven). Instead, some consider it more likely that he had the divine encounter recorded in 2 Corinthians 12 during the three years he spent in Arabia (Galatians 1:17–18). Another possibility is in Acts 14, where we read that the Iconians stoned him, meaning they threw heavy boulders and crushed him: "Jews came . . . from Antioch and Iconium and won over the crowds. Then they stoned Paul and dragged him out of the city, supposing that he was dead" (14:19). The disciples gathered around Paul, and somehow he got up and went on to the city of Derbe.

Whatever happened in that stoning must have been an unforgettable experience. Paul also writes of being shipwrecked, beaten, and involved in a wide variety of dangerous, fearsome happenings. In short, we have no idea when the great apostle had his most powerful encounter with the Holy. We can assume it was something that took place long after he had begun his service to Jesus Christ.

An interesting fact is that Paul reluctantly recounts this experience; he does so only because he has to defend his apostleship. In chapters 10 through 12 of 2 Corinthians, Paul stands against false teachings and accusations and seems even to have to defend his leadership among his own converts. In the midst of these apologies, he offers a brief but extremely revealing experience, and the "person" he refers to is obviously himself:

It is necessary to boast; nothing is to be gained by it, but I will go on to visions and revelations of the Lord. I know a person in Christ who fourteen years ago was caught up to the third heaven—whether in the body or out of the body I do not know; God knows—was caught up into Paradise and heard things that are not to be told, that no mortal is permitted to repeat. (2 Corinthians 12:1–4)

As Paul reluctantly writes of the experience, he refers to the "exceptional character of the revelations" (12:7). Then he adds:

Therefore, to keep me from being too elated, a thorn was given me in the flesh, a messenger of Satan to torment me, to keep me from being too elated. Three times I appealed to the Lord about this, that it would leave me, but [God] said to me, "My grace is sufficient for you, for my power is made perfect in weakness" (12:7–9).

There we have the account of this Holy encounter, but we still don't know or understand what happened. Paul uses language to let us know it was intense and far beyond the normal experience of Christians. But that's as far as he'll go in revealing what it was.

He speaks of having a thorn in the flesh—a subject of argument and discussion. The word translated *thorn* in the Greek is *skolps*. Although it can refer to a thorn, a more likely meaning is *stake*. It's as if Paul is saying he had been impaled on a sharp spike.

Most of the arguments and explanations of his thorn or stake center around some kind of physical malady. It's possible he had weak eyes, or had bad headaches, or was epileptic. No one knows. *I'm inclined to believe this was purely a spiritual issue.*[1]

Too many have found it convenient to focus on some kind of physical shortcoming and miss the point that Paul wants to make to the Corinthians. Regardless of what this stake or thorn is, the purpose is to humble him. He's not to glory in the results or in his exalted status.

Because Paul chooses not to reveal what it is, perhaps it's wise not to focus on identifying the *skolps* but to ask, "Okay, so what? How did all of this affect him?" Let's look at Paul and consider what he was trying to say to his readers. For me, his encounter with the Divine Pursuer went beyond words for him to express. Even more, whatever happened was so profound that he is unwilling to share details. He had revelations and understanding that are beyond those of ordinary people.

This reminds me that during the early days of my Christian experience, I read a biography of D. L. Moody. One time he was walking along the street, and something happened to him that was so powerful he said he could not talk about it but implied that it was something similar to what Paul must have referred to. When Paul speaks of ascending to the third heaven, it isn't a matter of counting or saying he got to the third of the seven. I think it means that it was totally and utterly beyond anything he had experienced before. Perhaps in the case of Paul, we might do better to focus on the results of the divine encounter instead of the cause of it.

A few paragraphs before he tells us of his third-heaven experience, he gets tired of hearing the boastings of false apostles and those who belittle his ministry, so he compares himself with them:

> Are they ministers of Christ? I am talking like a madman—I am a better one: with far greater labors, far more imprisonments, with countless floggings, and often near death. Five times I have received from the Jews forty lashes minus one. Three times I was beaten with rods. Once I received a stoning. Three times I was shipwrecked; for a night and a day I was adrift at sea; on frequent journeys, in danger from rivers, danger from bandits, danger from my own people, danger from Gentiles, danger in the city, danger in the wilderness, danger at sea, danger from false brothers and sisters; in toil and hardship, through many a sleepless night, hungry and thirsty, often without food, cold, and naked. And, besides other things, I am under daily pressure because of my anxiety for all the churches. (2 Corinthians 11:23–28)

It was forty lashes minus one because people believed that forty would kill a person; thirty-nine was the maximum anyone could receive. Paul points out that he has faced death and the worst possible human dangers countless times.

When I read such an account, and then it's followed by his revelation of going to the third heaven, I can only assume that something changed Paul, that the Relentless One grabbed him. He had long been a follower of Jesus. Many of those experiences took place during that fourteen-year period before he wrote—certainly before he ever visited Corinth.

Doesn't it make sense that Paul's encounter fortified him for every hardship and privation that he would have to face for Jesus Christ during the rest of his ministry? Wouldn't it have been a powerful experience for the Relentless God to have grabbed him, strengthened, and encouraged him so that when the worst hardships came, Paul would be ready? Isn't it possible that the Spirit removed all doubts and questions and feelings of inadequacy?

I wonder if part of Paul's dis-ease in writing to Corinth was that he hated to have to defend himself and his apostleship. If we follow his journeys in Acts, when he moves into a new place, he simply enters a city. As a Jew, on the first Sabbath he visits the synagogue, and when given the opportunity to speak, he stands up and speaks boldly about Jesus. When they chase him out of the synagogue, Paul goes to Gentiles or anyone who will listen. He makes no claims for apostolic authority, divine anointing, or spiritual commission. He speaks about God sending a Savior to the world.

Here's where I'm taking this: Paul preached effectively. Sometimes a riot ensued because of the opposition to his message, yet even before agitators and adversaries mobbed him, he already had a large gathering of people around him, listening. Many believed and turned to Jesus Christ.

Why would they do that? What would make them leave their heathen ways, the culture of their own people, and turn to a new faith? Paul was the reason. He stood before them as a living example of divine grace in a human being.

When we are filled with the grace of God, it shows. Most people will acknowledge this, even though we're not sure how to explain it. There's one amazing example in Numbers where Moses went up into the mountain to be alone with God, and when he returned, the people were terrified because his face shone. The brightness of his visage glowed so strongly that they made him put a veil over it.

We assume that is a literal statement. But what if it's not? What if it's a change in Moses that's so profound people sense that he has come back completely different? What if the brightness isn't as literal as it is spiritual? What if they sensed the power of God so strongly that they couldn't bear to have Moses stare into their eyes?

The only illustration I can give of such an effect is of a student I knew during my college days. He walked with God, and there was an aura—for lack of a better term—that many of us recognized. He was as fully committed to Jesus Christ as anyone I knew. Several times he would go to one of the students alone and say something—a few words that would bring conviction. He would speak of things that weren't obvious and that the rest of us wouldn't be aware of. When he did, the person who heard him responded in astonishment, sometimes in tears.

A friend named Victoria told me that she avoided him: "When he looks at me, I have the feeling that he can see into my soul." (We later learned some things about her that explained why she was afraid to be around him.)

I'm not sure that's the best way to try to explain Paul. My sense is that he was in such an intimate divine relationship that when he spoke those who were listening heard him as though he spoke directly from the Holy Spirit.

⟋⟍

One biblical account that hints of this is in Acts 5, and it happens shortly after the initial forming of the early church. Converts sold their goods, brought the money to the apostles, and lived in a kind of communal relationship. One couple, Ananias and Sapphira, had property that they sold, but they brought only part of the money to Peter. In bringing a partial gift, they as much as lied, claiming it was everything they had received.

Peter immediately asked,

> Why has Satan filled your heart to lie to the Holy Spirit and to keep back part of the proceeds of the land? While it remained unsold, did it not remain your own? And after it was sold, were not the proceeds at your disposal? How is it that you have contrived this deed in your heart? You did not lie to us but to God! (Acts 5:3–4)

How did Peter know they had lied? He may have seen it in their eyes, or someone may have told him. The biblical account, however, reads as if God revealed this information to Peter in some kind of special, supernatural way.

One personal experience gives me a sense of how this operates. During our years in Africa, we worked mostly with the Luo tribe, the second largest in Kenya. I also felt a deep concern for the Asians who lived in a remote section near Lake Victoria. They were the businesspeople who owned small shops where people bought anything from cloth to coffee to cooking oil. Most of them were Hindu, with a minority being Muslim.

Mr. Yusuf, a Muslim, was the teacher of a one-room school for Asian children. We met during the first week after I moved into the area, and he treated me rudely. I didn't take it as a personal affront; I sensed that he was either antagonistic toward me as a white man or to the message I brought.

I didn't try to talk to him about God then or later because I sensed he wouldn't listen anyway. Whenever I saw him, I waved, smiled, and occasionally we'd chat about world events. At least a year went by, and we saw each other from time to time when I visited the Asian shops, but we never had any lengthy or personal conversation.

One day Mr. Yusuf stopped me and confessed, "I don't know your God, and I don't think I could see him, but if I did see him, I think he would smile the way you do."

Tears filled my eyes as I stood in front of him—speechless, shocked, and amazed. The rest of our conversation remains a blur to me, but after I walked away, I kept wondering what I had said or done to provoke such a positive response. I could think of nothing.

Then I realized this was grace at work. From that day on the teacher and I became friends. He invited me to his home and asked me about the Bible and about Jesus. One day he told me that he believed in Jesus Christ as the Savior. Shortly after that he asked Shirley and me to teach the Bible in his school. He and other Asians regularly attended our conferences.

Although that experience happened years ago, it still burns powerfully within my heart. Somehow the Relentless Pursuer chased that man. It wasn't my words, my charm, or my great wisdom that enabled Mr. Yusuf to see the smile of God. I think the Holy One had pursued him for a long time, grabbed him, and simply wouldn't let go.

Because of my experience and what I read elsewhere in the Bible, I get a glimpse of the power of the Holy invasion of human lives. It also helps me to get a little closer to the results of Paul's encounter. He became an utterly fearless servant, and no ordeal was too much for him, no challenge too great. The encounter he had is the type not often spoken of in the church and probably not well known. Writings of some of the mystics hint of this kind of relationship with God, but it's certainly not the experience of all or even of many, and it probably won't be the experience of many who read this.

What we can learn from Paul's example is the unlimited power from on high that works in the lives of others. We instinctively recognize that power when we talk with those rare and special people. We sense something out of the ordinary with them. They have a special quality about them that makes them stand out and exemplify Jesus Christ. The Holy has gripped them, held them, and continues to push them onward. We can't explain it, and we don't find words that adequately communicate the spiritual mystique—and yet we know it's there.

It's that inner sense of the holy presence that speaks through human lips. It's the voice that brings conviction because of the message and not the messenger. It's the touch of the Holy.

CHAPTER FOURTEEN

HOLY BELIEF

Years ago my friend Alvin and I attended a large meeting conducted by an evangelist named William Branham. He preached for more than an hour, and even though I had only been a believer for perhaps five years, I soon realized the evangelist probably didn't know as much about the Bible as I did. After he stopped preaching, however, he did an amazing thing: He called for the sick to come forward, and a large number of people rushed down the aisles.

Alvin and I sat in the next-to-last row, and although we couldn't see everything clearly, we heard everything. Mr. Branham prayed, sometimes laying his hand on a forehead, and said, "Be healed!" In a couple of instances as people came toward him, he called out their names or addresses. He even yelled out the Social Security number of one man.

As we witnessed the next forty-five minutes of the healing

service, Alvin and I had quite different reactions. "He's got people in the audience who tell him those things," Alvin whispered. When a large woman raised her arms and cried out that God had healed her of a serious heart condition, he snickered. "Wait until she goes to a doctor." (The woman said it was the first pain-free moment she had experienced in twelve years.) In the meantime, Alvin had a long litany of other negative remarks.

I want to present three other accounts before I comment on this one.

⁕

(1) A lengthy story appears in Acts 16 that most people consider recounts at least two miracles. In the city of Philippi in Macedonia, Paul and his entourage go to the river's edge and meet with a group of women gathered for prayer. The Bible says simply, "A certain woman named Lydia, a worshiper of God, was listening to us. . . . The Lord opened her heart to listen eagerly to what was said by Paul" (16:14). She believes and is baptized.

Paul and the others preach in Philippi, and later they cast a demon out of a fortune-teller. In response, the owners of the delivered woman have Paul and Silas imprisoned. At midnight a violent earthquake takes place, knocks down the doors, and breaks the chains on the prisoners, yet no one is hurt or tries to escape. The guard awakens and rushes in, sees the effect of the disaster, falls on his knees, and cries out,

"What must I do to be saved?" (16:30).

Not long ago I read the comments on that passage by a well-credentialed scholar. He dismissed the healing of the fortune-teller by arguing that Paul's acceptance of her and his show of compassion was all she needed to act normal. Then he spent nearly two pages denying the miracle in the prison. His major argument pointed out that earthquakes were common in that area. For him, the entire thing was a natural disaster and certainly no miracle.

(2) After Paul and 253 other people were shipwrecked, all of them landed safely on the island of Malta. While Paul gathers wood, a poisonous snake clamps onto him. When the others see it, they're convinced that he's evil, or else the viper wouldn't have struck him. Paul astonishes them when he shakes off the deadly creature and goes on with his task. When he's not harmed, the people go to the opposite extreme: "They changed their minds and began to say that he was a god" (Acts 28:6).

Some scholars have said that the nationals mistakenly assumed the snake was poisonous because it looked similar to one that was.

(3) A woman in a remote village in Kenya gave birth and began to hemorrhage. Nothing would stop her bleeding. They had no medical facilities anywhere in the region, so her husband called for the elders, who came to their house and petitioned the Lord. The woman died, but they continued to pray: "For seven hours we knelt beside her, and then she came back to life. She opened her eyes, and the bleeding had stopped.

God had healed her in answer to our prayers." An evangelist wrote these words to us in Luo, the tribal language.

We read the letter to a group of missionaries, translating it as we read. One of the women, who spoke Luo, said, "Oh, she didn't die. She was just unconscious." She pointed out that the word *tho* ("died") could also mean being in a coma or not responding, as well as dead. She was accurate about the language. Was she also accurate in insisting that the woman merely recovered naturally and wasn't miraculously healed?

In all of these accounts, something happens that most of us call miracles. Or we could take a different approach and explain them away. Which interpretation is correct? Did God use Mr. Branham to heal people? Was he a fake and thus an unscrupulous man who took advantage of hurting souls? Are the fortune-teller's healing and the earthquake story in Acts 16 meant to be taken as demonstrations of divine power? Had the freed woman been delusional? Was it a temporary deliverance? If the earthquake is a miracle, then God overruled natural law by supernatural action. If it was merely a natural event, as the scholar insisted, the best we could say is that the timing puts the earthquake into the category of an unusual happening or circumstance.

I'm not going to answer; instead I want to point out a principle I call Holy Belief.

Take any miraculous story in the Bible. For example, crit-
ics have long jeered at the parting of the waters of the Red
Sea, the falling of the walls of Jericho, or the stretching of a
boy's meager lunch to feed thousands. Did they literally happen? If those events happened today, could we explain them
through natural events? Or did natural events come into play
that ancients didn't understand but that we could easily
explain today?

We have no way of answering, of course, so the final word
comes down to a matter of faith. Who argues that? Although
the naïve see miracles everywhere they go, skeptics see only
the laws of nature operating. Most of us probably stand somewhere between the two extremes. Yes, it's a matter of faith.

What if we consider these from a divine point of view?
Suppose we look at such happenings as the Holy One pursuing people and opening them to the message. (I have neither
the expertise nor the inclination to debate why some respond
and others don't. As one who came to the faith as an adult, I
think anytime anyone turns to Jesus Christ and believes, it's
an exciting miracle.)

Think about the story of the earthquake. The Philippian
jailer heard the crumbling walls, saw the prisoners' chains
gone, and fear filled his heart. He accepted what his senses
told him and refused to take refuge in natural explanations.
Even more delightful is the way he responds after he believed.

The story begins within the prison at Philippi. Paul and
Silas refuse to sulk or complain after being wrongly incarcer-
ated; by now these two men had come to accept that anything

that happened in their lives was of God's orchestration. For example, just before they went to Macedonia, God had spoken to Paul:

> During the night Paul had a vision: there stood a man of Macedonia pleading with him and saying, "Come over to Macedonia and help us." When he had seen the vision, we [Luke was traveling with them] immediately tried to cross over to Macedonia, being convinced that God had called us to proclaim the good news to them. (Acts 16:9–10)

They haven't had an easy time before this, undergoing all kinds of persecution. They were ready to pay whatever price God demanded of them. Now they're arrested, and Luke prepares us for the end of the story:

> The crowd joined in attacking them, and the magistrates had them stripped of their clothing and ordered them to be beaten with rods. After they had given them a severe flogging, they threw them into the prison and ordered the jailer to keep them securely. Following these instructions, he put them in the innermost cell and fastened their feet in the stocks. (16:22–24)

In jail they pray and sing, and Luke says that the other prisoners listened. "Suddenly there was an earthquake, so violent that the foundations of the prison were shaken . . . and everyone's chains were unfastened" (16:26).

Apparently the guard has gone to sleep during the singing; the earthquake awakens him. He rushes in. The place is dark and his obvious assumption is that his two main prisoners have fled. Under Roman law, if a prisoner escaped, the jailer suffered the punishment the prisoner would have endured, so killing himself seems to be a sensible solution. The jailer pulls out his sword to end his life.

> But Paul shouted in a loud voice, "Do not harm yourself, for we are all here." The jailer called for lights, and rushing in, he fell down trembling before Paul and Silas. Then he brought them outside and said, "Sirs, what must I do to be saved?" They answered, "Believe on the Lord Jesus, and you will be saved, you and your household." They spoke the word of the Lord to him and to all who were in his house. (16:28–32)

In this powerful account, the jailer faces his own death for wrongly believing he had allowed the prisoners to escape. Now he grasps the situation. Although the building is in ruins and the manacles are broken, the prisoners have not gone anywhere.

This is the moment where I see the decisive hand of the Holy touching the guard. Isn't it amazing that he had previously met Paul and Silas and nothing happened to him? The two preachers had been badly beaten before being brought to the prison. Even in the midst of their physical pain—which must have been considerable—the man dutifully locks them down.

Later that same night the jailer sleeps in a remote part of

the prison, while Paul and Silas sing praises; some of the noise must have disturbed the diligent man. When the earthquake occurs, however, something transforms his life.

Now the jailer believes. Even if they had frequent earthquakes, his knowledge of natural catastrophes didn't seem to hinder his ability to accept the miracle. The Pursuing One broke into the man's life through this incident. Beyond the astounding effects of the earthquake—destroying the doors and the chains—is the fact that no one is hurt. In that instant faith burns within the jailer. He falls on his knees and asks the crucial question: "What must I do?"

"Believe in Jesus Christ," Paul tells him. How simple; but that's all it takes. Obviously from the context, they didn't stop with that simple statement but continued to speak to him about God. They moved on to instructing him, and he became a convert. In that instant he was a believer—he made a full commitment.

The story ends with the jailer washing their wounds and providing food for the former prisoners. He and his entire family are baptized, and this becomes their public confession of faith in Jesus Christ. Within hours Paul and Silas went from dangerous prisoners in the eyes of the jailer to intimate friends. No longer enemies, they are now brothers in the Lord.

The passage closes with these words: "He and his entire household rejoiced that he had become a believer in God" (16:34).

Although one of the most dramatic scenes of the New Testament, this narrative, perhaps as well as any other, helps us to see what happens when the Holy redemptively encounters sinful people. In the instant of God's touch, their lives are changed forever.

Nothing makes the conversion story—and Holy Belief—clearer than the actions of the jailer *after* he believes. He follows through with changes that support his affirmation of faith. It's not simply a matter of his saying, "I believe." He is altered. What a lowly and loathsome task it must have been for him to personally clean the wounds of his prisoners. The two men he was to guard carefully now give him the words of life to follow.

He receives water baptism and invites the prisoners into his home, offering them food. The Bible doesn't say where or how they slept, but I'm sure it would be safe to say that Paul and Silas remained in the guard's own house. He had been changed; he received the touch of the Holy, and he believed.

Regardless of whether some explain the earthquake as a merely natural occurrence, even more important than the incident itself is the result. It's the "afterward" statement of such stories that speaks the most loudly. Many people can speak of powerful, even miraculous, moments of supernatural intervention in their lives. But the story isn't complete until they answer one simple question: So what?

Then they must ask, "How has it impacted my life? Did I sense the touch of the Holy in such a way that I haven't been the same? Did the event establish or deepen my belief in the

God who constantly seeks us?" Another way to think of this is to focus on the Relentless Pursuer. To what lengths will God go to impact our lives?

Isn't it possible that some of us (and perhaps all of us) have those momentary blips of insight that build on each other? Each experience marks the persistent touch of the Divine Chaser, but we pull away, unwilling to be caught. Isn't it likely that we have a dozen things in our lives that the Holy Spirit wants to change, but doesn't do everything at once? Could it be that we move forward, ignorant of many short-comings and spiritual needs that the Relentless One isn't ready to confront us with *yet*?

The good news is that the Pursuer doesn't give up and keeps after us. Of course, there are biblical stories of those who crossed the line and totally refused divine grace, such as Judas. But what about those of us who are "in the faith"? What are the divine pursuits going on in us right now?

Isn't it highly probable that as we walk in fellowship with Jesus Christ, there may yet be parts of us that race in the opposite direction? Isn't it likely that we may be enjoying the showers of blessings and withholding ourselves from God— unconsciously? Isn't it possible that the Holy Belief that grabs and holds us may be those special moments when God finally says, "Enough"?

I think so.

In the final chapter, I want to share an experience that fits into this category.

PREPARING TO BE FOUND

T ell me *how*," I remember demanding of the teacher of our Sunday school class. At the time I had been a believer for about a year, and that encounter exemplifies one of the first problems I had in the faith—learning the "secret code language" of Christians, the use of terms that made little sense to someone who had recently come in from the outside. She had just said that in order to grow we must "yield our lives to God."

"How do I yield?" I asked.

"You just lay it all on the Cross of Calvary."

I shook my head; the words made no sense to me. "But how—how do I do that?"

"You surrender everything to God."

"How?"

"You—you just give it all up."

"But *how*?"

By then she was exasperated with me. She may have thought I was trying to annoy her or that I was acting dense. I wasn't; I simply wanted a simple answer to my one-word question: How?

"Well, if you don't know, I'm sure I can't help you," she replied, and moved on to a different topic.

That response shocked me, and her attitude irritated me. I was a sincere seeker after truth, and she cut me off.

As the years have passed, however, I think she may have given me the correct answer. That is, she couldn't help me. Any step of growth in the Christian life was something I had to learn by myself. I had to figure out things that no teacher could ever explain satisfactorily.

And now, decades later, I'm back to that same question: *How?* How do we prepare ourselves so that the Relentless One can break into our lives and change us? And then break in again and keep on changing us? How do we open up so that the Spirit can show us truths about ourselves that we never saw before? How can we position ourselves for God to grant us insight that shatters old images and brings us into greater light and into a more intimate, holy relationship?

This is the most honest answer I can offer: When we live as faithfully as we can; that's all we can do. It's up to the Holy Spirit, and despite all our efforts, this falls into the area of divine responsibility. We can't make ourselves holier. In fact, when we insist on knowing how, aren't we moving into old patterns of taking control of our lives? Of asserting responsibility for that which is divine prerogative? Of insisting that we're in charge of our own destiny?

If God is sovereign (a given in my theological framework), we can't prepare, plan, program, or negotiate. We can be aware that the Holy Spirit takes the initiative and invades our world so we don't have to be struck mute like Zechariah. Even so, most of all, we have absolutely no idea what God is going to do next.

For example, Jesus' final words to his disciples before his ascension were that they were to "stay here in the city until you have been clothed with power from on high" (Luke 24:49). We have no idea what they expected, but on the day of Pentecost, Peter was as surprised as anyone by the marvelous outpouring of the Holy Spirit. There is absolutely no way we can figure where or how or when the Spirit will invade, challenge, or chase. What we can do is pray for God to keep us open. We can listen for the softest tones of the Spirit in the quiet hours of the night.

Earlier in this book, I told of my experience when the Holy Spirit used a type of personality test to push me to face myself. I endured misery and feelings of shame as I first denied and then tried to absorb what God pushed me into. That "forced entry" ushered in changes. Through biblical incidents, I've tried to illustrate that God is and always has been the Breaking-Into-Human-Lives-One—and these events occur at the most unexpected moments. I've also tried to point to the Relentless Pursuer, the One who won't let go.

I can suggest no way to make this happen; however, I can suggest a way to live. If we continue to seek God daily, if we respond when we feel the divine nudge, we're in a place of readiness. Then it's up to the Holy One to break in. The pursuit isn't over and will never be over until we see the literal face of Jesus and hear him say, "Well done, good and faithful servant."

No, I can't tell anyone *how* any more than the Sunday school teacher of long ago could tell me. If we remind ourselves that God has chosen us and part of that choosing involves loving us, seeking out the best for us, and not giving up no matter how much we resist, we're traveling along the right path.

The pursuit never stops because the divine work is never finished in us. No matter what level of spirituality we may attain (or think we've attained), the Holy Spirit pursues and begs us not to give up. We find a hunger, a desire for "something more" in our lives.

Rather than explain how the Pursuer functions or try to explain how to find that illusive "something more," the best I can do is share one more story in my life of an encounter with the Relentless One.

This is a recent event, and I'm sharing it as a person who was pursued, found, and has been held tightly by the divine embrace for most of my adult years. I've been around long enough and have had enough experiences that I'd like to think I no longer need any divine force to pursue me. That's not the case, of course, but once in a while I ask myself, "Shouldn't I have it all worked out by now? Shouldn't I be the example of those who race toward the Relentless One instead of being one of those who is chased?"

"How can it be," I've asked myself, "that despite all these years of commitment, I still find ways to run away, hide, deny, or ignore the tender touches of my loving heavenly Father?" My only answer is that the sin factor always remains within me. As part of the sinful nature, I have developed an extremely efficient capacity for self-delusion. It is unfortunate, but until I utter the final "amen" in this life, I won't lose that ability.

I'm recording this story, which wasn't part of the original manuscript. My almost-relentless editor, Christopher Soderstrom, asked me to strengthen the ending. He said it needed "an infusion of passion—a little more from your heart."

A little more? I protested silently when I read his message. *How can there be more? Haven't I already stripped myself naked? How much of my emotional guts do I need to spill? What more can I offer to encourage or help others?*

For five days I resisted, until finally I decided there was one story I needed to tell. I don't enjoy exposing my spiritual nakedness, and like Adam, this experience still makes me want to hide behind a garment of fig leaves. It's also an "afterward" story that makes it all worthwhile.

I'm sharing this account to illustrate that in spite of the years I've called myself a practicing or committed Christian, despite my dedication and countless times of surrender, every once in a while the Holy One still needs to pursue me.

In the early 1980s I resigned from the pastorate of a growing, successful congregation to become a full-time writer. For eight years I had been writing and publishing articles and books. A year before I resigned, the senior editor of a publishing house contacted me and asked me to ghostwrite the autobiography of a then-famous singer. I happily agreed, enjoyed the process, and the publishing house liked my work. They asked me to do more books for them.

A ghostwriter remains anonymous, and at first the concept troubled me. I wrestled with this question: *Can I write for God and not care who gets the credit?* My ego was big enough and my self-esteem weak enough that it wasn't easy for me to say yes. Once I said, "I surrender," I knew it was the right thing.

Thus I became a full-time ghostwriter, and I liked what I did. The pay was good, and I didn't have to generate publicity or make public appearances. More ghostwriting projects came along, and I said yes with eagerness. It was, for me, a wonderful life. I wanted to write, and this suited me.

Once I jumped into full-time ghostwriting, I did not write a book of my own for ten years. The editor who first asked me to ghostwrite kept me busy, and I did thirty-five books for his publishing house. Other editors heard about my work and contacted me. What I didn't realize is that even though God had pushed me into ghostwriting, remaining a ghost wasn't the end of the divine plan for my life.

I didn't understand this, of course. More accurately, I didn't want to understand. My wife, however, sensed ghost-writing was a part-time ministry. Occasionally she'd touch my cheek or hug me and say gently, "I wish you'd also write your own books." I loved her being ambitious for me, but I made no effort to write my own material.

"I don't have anything to say," was my usual answer. An even stronger argument was that the book opportunities were coming in rapidly, and most of them were Christian books on a wide variety of topics. I stayed so busy producing books for other people that I had no chance to think about whether I had anything to say. (That was my form of running, but I wasn't spiritually astute enough to grasp that.)

Once or twice God sneaked someone into my life who casually asked, "Why don't you write your own books?" I didn't seriously ponder their question. "This is where God put me" was my answer. And who would argue with me over that statement?

As a ghostwriter, most of the time my name didn't appear in the book. Sometimes the "author" acknowledged my help with a line such as "Thanks to Cec Murphey for his assis-tance." One celebrity thanked me for "writing a draft" of his book. I didn't mind, because once I made the commitment to write and not care who received credit, my name on the book became a non-issue.

In the mid–1990s, however, a crisis of conscience con-fronted me. I wrote the autobiography of a famous person, and the book received a prestigious award. The author never thanked me and neither did the publishing house. Even my agent at the time remained silent. This pushed me into an ethical dilemma.

My issue was no longer one of not caring about credit. Instead I asked, "Am I participating in an unethical act—which makes this sinful?" That sounds strong, but I realized I had helped to perpetuate *a lie*—and I had done it many times.

When readers bought ghostwritten books, they assumed the celebrity had written every word. Because my name didn't appear on the title page, I had willingly participated in the deception.

I tell this story because God was in pursuit and I didn't know it. Or perhaps more accurately, I wasn't open to hearing the voice that called out to me. After all, this was ministry, and I was serving Jesus Christ.

Or as I said in the previous chapter, maybe it was a matter of belief. The Pursuer tapped my shoulder a number of times, but I pushed away the divine intervention. Because I *knew* what the Holy Spirit had called me to do, I didn't hear or believe any of those quiet interruptions.

"When are you going to write your own books?" began to be a question friends asked me more frequently. I finally admitted that God might be speaking, and I decided to do something about it. In retrospect, I think of myself as the person described in James 1:22–24:

> And remember, it is a message to obey, not just to listen to. If you don't obey, you are only fooling yourself.

For if you just listen and don't obey, it is like looking at your face in a mirror but doing nothing to improve your appearance. *You see yourself, walk away, and forget what you look like.* (NLT, emphasis mine)

I didn't want to hear people talk that way.

I didn't want to believe this message came to me from heaven.

"When are you going to write your own books?" I hated that question. I hated it even more because my best friend, David, began to ask it on a regular basis. He's not a writer, so I patiently explained to him that the writing business wasn't like other professions. He accepted my answer, but he didn't believe me.

For several weeks I went through an extremely difficult time. My new agent, Deidre Knight, helped me with the first part. She said, "From now on, if you don't get credit on the cover, you don't write." (Today my name appears after the "author," followed by the word *with* to designate me as the writer.) Within weeks after we made that decision, we turned down an excellent writing opportunity because the celebrity refused to put my name on the book beneath his.

This story isn't to speak against those for whom I've written. Until recent years the publishing industry had not named ghostwriters because they believed the books would sell better. This story is to point out that God refused to allow me to rationalize, and the Divine Pursuer chased me until I hit the dead end and crashed into a stone wall.

I didn't want to write my "stuff." What did I have to say that others had not said better? Not only had I filled my life and thrown my energies into writing books for others, but I had also denied my own voice. Although I never actually wrote a list, I came up with seven or eight reasons not to write my material.

After a very weary time, I felt a bit like Jonah, who "rose up to flee . . . from the presence of the LORD" (Jonah 1:3 KJV). Finally I promised God I'd stop running. Just before I changed agents I wrote a book, and my then-agent sold it to a small publisher. The book did not sell many copies, and I assumed this fact set me free.

Writing one book, however, didn't free me from the Persistent, Relentless Pursuer. I felt as if I had no choice—I had to write my material from my heart. I raised every argument I knew to convince myself otherwise. Jesus and I took long walks together every day, and I carefully, patiently explained why I was obviously not hearing the voice of the Spirit. I threw in words about my material being self-indulgent, boring, and mawkish. I became rather skillful at rebuking my self-aggrandizing nature for wanting *my* name on the cover.

Finally, to shut up the persistent voice, I did start writing a few of my own books, but I did all of them between major assignments of ghostwriting. My ghosted books continued to sell far better than my own.

But this story is about encountering the One-Who-Won't-Let-Me-Go. The encounter came about because my friend David and I had talked about going to Antarctica for a long time. During the 1990s I had ghostwritten two secular books that involved the white continent, and I wanted to go there myself.

We joined forty-six others going to Antarctica aboard a small Russian ship. One day we landed on Deception Island, off the Antarctic Peninsula. Intentionally I walked away from everyone else to be alone.

I found an isolated spot where Waddell seals lazed on the ice. Penguins waddled past me. As I stared at the azure skies and the pristine white of icebergs, scavenger skuas circled several young penguins. A strong, freezing wind ripped through my clothes. I shivered and pulled my fleece-lined cap tighter over my ears, but I didn't move.

As I stared at my surroundings, the Holy Spirit nudged me in the deepest way possible. I heard no words, and I didn't even feel any emotional difference. In that moment I knew what I had to do. I admitted that part of me had been running for years. The fleeing was finally over. The divine lasso had tightened, and at last I stopped fighting.

An encouraging factor to me is that shortly after my return from Antarctica, Carolyn Driver called me. She heads Christ Discipleship Ministries, and the group prays regularly for me. "I want to know what happened to you in Antarctica," she said without any introduction. She informed me that she had been praying for me, and every time she closed her eyes she saw me standing near penguins: "And I knew God was speaking to you."

If I hadn't been positive before, I was now. Cec Murphey had to make changes. Since that trip to the white continent, I've followed through. For instance, I've turned down several lucrative projects. Yes, I worried a little about my finances, but the holy peace I felt assured me I was doing the right thing. The smiles on the faces of my wife and my best friend reinforced that conviction. For several years they had heard the message that now the Untiring, Relentless One had finally gotten through to me.

⌘

I cringed inside while I wrote this story. Four times today I've angrily walked away from my computer and yelled back at it, "Who wants to read this junk?" I'm writing it anyway, because I'm supposed to be among the mature believers, those who blissfully move at the slightest nod of the Spirit and fol-low after only the slightest whisper. Well, perhaps *they* do. Instead, as I share this, I repeat a message I used to hear often in the late 1970s: "Please be patient. God isn't finished with me yet."

The Relentless Pursuer isn't through with me. The Per-sistent God pursues me and just won't let go.

This doesn't give much practical advice on being pursued by the Holy, but I'm not sure anyone can. Perhaps the best I can offer is the prayer of Richard of Chicester (c. 1197–1253):

Day by day, Dear Lord,
of Thee three things I pray:
To see Thee more clearly,
Love Thee more dearly,
Follow Thee more nearly,
Day by day.[1]

The right heart attitude helps us ready ourselves for a new pursuit by the Lovingly Relentless One. Despite the pain, confusion, and uncertainty, we know that we are still under divine construction. We're becoming the holiest possible habitat for the Holy Spirit.

Here's a prayer I wrote in my journal in January of 2002:

Take away my resistance. Every day, enable me to reach toward you instead of run from you. Because I know you won't ever give up, each time the lasso tightens around my neck I'm learning to stop. Fighting or running no longer works. Although I can't explain how, I'm learning to yield. And when I start to complain, I'm reminded that you love me so deeply you just won't let me get away with anything that displeases you. For this I'm grateful. Amen.

This relentless pursuit is an ongoing chase by God—one that ends only when our life does.

ENDNOTES

INTRODUCTION

1. Cecil Murphey, *The God Who Pursues: Encountering a Relentless God* (Minneapolis: Bethany House, 2002).

CHAPTER NINE

1. Isaac Watts, "Jesus Shall Reign Where'er the Sun" (1719).

CHAPTER THIRTEEN

1. The word translated *flesh* (Greek: *sarx*) has several meanings, and it can refer to the body; however, most of the uses of *sarx* in the New Testament refer to the sinful, carnal, or lower nature (e.g., Galatians 5:17; Jude 23; Romans 8:3, 5; 1 John 2:16; 1 Peter 2:10). This, then, leaves open the identity of Paul's thorn.

CHAPTER FIFTEEN

1. "Day by Day, Dear Lord," as found in *The Hymnbook* (Richmond, Va.: Presbyterian Church in the United States, 1958), 541.

Life-Changing Journeys
for the Heart and Mind!

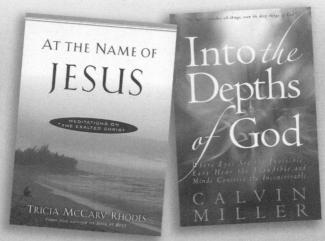

Putting Jesus Back at the Center of Faith

Understanding, studying, and claiming the names of Jesus will lead readers to experience His presence in their lives in new and unexpected ways. Rather than a how-to book, *At the Name of Jesus* focuses on the awesome reality in the promises suggested by the names of our Savior: Redeemer, Deliverer, Lord of Glory, and more. Rhodes' passion inspires readers to respond to God's call with wonder, joy, delight, and awe.

At the Name of Jesus by Tricia McCary Rhodes

Hunger No More

The waters of life are rough—at the surface. Beneath the choppy waves of circumstances is a peaceful, unchanging dwelling place in God. For those desiring a deep relationship with God, Calvin Miller shows how to break the tyranny of things that occupy the mind and discover intimacy with God. Entering the depths of the fullness of God is not some distant thing for which a Christian must struggle throughout life. It is as near as one's heart!

Into the Depths of God by Calvin Miller

Available at your bookstore or by calling 1-866-241-6733.
(Please mention BOBIA)

BETHANY HOUSE
11400 Hampshire Ave. S., Minneapolis, MN 55438
www.bethanyhouse.com